THE
RAMBAM

The Story of
Rabbi Moshe ben Maimon

THE
RAMBAM

The Story of
Rabbi Moshe ben Maimon

by
Yaacov Dovid Shulman

C.I.S. PUBLISHERS
New York • London • Jerusalem

Published and distributed
in the U.S., Canada and overseas by
C.I.S. Publishers and Distributors
180 Park Avenue, Lakewood, New Jersey 08701
(908) 905-3000 Fax: (908) 367-6666

Distributed in Israel by
C.I.S. International (Israel)
Rechov Mishkalov 18
Har Nof, Jerusalem
Tel: 02-518-935

Distributed in the U.K. and Europe by
C.I.S. International (U.K.)
89 Craven Park Road
London N15 6AH, England
Tel: 81-809-3723

Book and cover design: Deenee Cohen
Typography: Nechamie Miller
Cover painting: James Gain

ISBN 1-56062-253-9 hard cover
1-56062-254-7 soft cover

PRINTED IN THE UNITED STATES OF AMERICA

Table of Contents

Preface

IT IS WITH A SENSE OF GREAT PRIVILEGE THAT I HAVE WRITTEN THIS biography of the leader of Israel, Rabbi Moshe ben Maimon.

Fortunately, a great deal of documentation exists that illuminates the life of the Rambam and his times.

The Rambam himself wrote many letters that reflect on his private circumstances, and these have been drawn on heavily. Among other documents that were preserved in the Cairo Genizah are personal letters to his brother, David, and to various friends, students and admirers

In addition, the Rambam was deeply involved in the public issues of his day, and many of his writings on these matters have survived.

Thus, it has been possible to present a portrait of the Rambam's private and public lie with the aid of a wealth of documentation.

The Rambam lived in fascinating times about which a great deal of information is available. It has been one of the purposes of this book to present a richly-detailed portrait of those times.

More than fifty books were used as source material in the writing of this book. Some of the most important material on the Rambam was found in the two-volume set of *Igros Harambam*, edited by Yitzchak Shailat. Other material was gleaned from such works as *Seder Hadoros*; *The Rishonim* by Rabbi Hirsch Goldwurm; *Hamoreh Ladoros* by Meir Uryan; *Rabbeinu Moshe ben Maimon* by A. Urinovski; and the children's book, *Harambam*, by N. T. Sifrai, which contains some very interesting source material about the life of the Rambam. In addition, translations of the Rambam's medical writings were consulted.

Books on many aspects of the background were used, among them: *Yemenite Jews*; *Atlas of the Jewish World*; *Saladin: A Biography*; *The Crusades*; *Egypt: Reflections on Continuity*; *Moorish Culture in Spain*; *The Genius of Arab Civilization*; *Islam and the Arab World*; *The Great Cities: Cairo*; *Morocco: Insights City Guide*; *Flora and Fauna in the Mediterranean*; and *Medieval Islamic Medicine*.

The reader might note the absence of various folk tales. These were not used because they were unsubstantiated. Also, there are disagreements over various details in the Rambam's life, such as the circumstances of his first marriage. This book has compared these various versions and attempted to present a reasonable chronology of events, taking into account both the Rambam's personal life and the background circumstances.

In working on this book, I gained a sense of the Rambam not only as a master of the Torah but as a man filled with the greatest love and compassion for all Jews, a man who risked his life on many occasions for their sake. It is my hope that this aspect of the Rambam's life is adequately expressed in this book.

May the merit of the Rambam, the Great Eagle, stand by me and by all Israel, until the laws of the Beis Hamikdash that he detailed in the *Mishneh Torah* are again applicable, may it be soon and in our day.

Yaacov Dovid Shulman
Shevat 5754

1

Rabbi Maimon

The following narrative was adapted from sefer Seder Hadoros. This work was written in the late 1600s by Rabbi Yechiel ben Shlomo Heilprin of Minsk, Lithuania. The Chida called the author "geon" and noted his "ability in Talmud and his great knowledge that leaves nothing hidden from him . . . One can recognize his greatness, for the Bavli and Yerushalmi and the Midrashim are all in his grasp. His overviews are astonishing and wonderful." [Shem Hagedolim] At times, Rabbi Heilprin quoted anecdotes about gedolim that he had read in other texts. Although their historical accuracy may be questioned, the fact that Rabbi Heilprin saw fit to include them in his Seder Hadoros lends them a certain presumption of veracity.

Rabbi Maimon walked across the Guadalquivir Bridge, barely noticing its graceful arches or the hundreds of colorful villas that lined the riverbank. A strikingly handsome man in his mid-forties, he looked abstracted and concerned. He stepped through the gate of the bridge and into Cordoba, heading for the Jewish quarter one mile to the north.

On the broad street, boys and old men led donkeys laden with grain, dyed silks and coffee. The scent of spices from China and India floated through the air. And from the upper story of a house came a snatch of poetry and the hypnotic lilt of a lute.

Rabbi Maimon passed an alley of jewelers, where earrings and bangles glittered in the soft, setting sun. In the next alley, bright swathes of silk, linen and cotton were spread out before the passersby.

A few steps further, the air was scented with cardamom and saffron. Dried cherries bulged from a fat burlap bag.

The owner of a saddler's shop approached him eagerly, his chin raised.

"Honored rabbi, come see my fine wares!"

Rabbi Maimon was shaken from his thoughts.

"You are most kind," he answered in courtly Arabic. "At another time, I shall avail myself of your fine merchandise." He hurried along the street, and the merchant's smile disappeared.

At last, Rabbi Maimon arrived at Cordoba's chief synagogue. Jews were bustling into the tall, stone building, wearing striped, rectangular tunics with wide sleeves over long shirts and trousers. Some of the men wore turbans, others embroidered caps.

Rabbi Maimon walked into the synagogue and unwrapped the scarf that had been wrapped about his turbaned head and shoulders.

A man stepped up to him and for a long moment grasped his right hand with two hands. "Rabbi Maimon!"

Rabbi Maimon recognized Yitzchak Tzadiki, an old friend

and a royal minter. He reached his left hand out so that the two men were clasping their four hands. "It is a pleasure to see you!" Yitzchak Tzadiki placed his right hand next to his heart as a sign of his sincerity.

"The pleasure is truly mine." Rabbi Maimon too placed his hand on his heart. "What are you doing here? I thought that you are learning in Lucena under Rabbi Yosef ibn Migash."

At the *bimah*, the cantor began chanting, *"Ashrei yoshvei veisecha!"*

The congregation began the silent *Amidah*. Sunlight shone brilliantly on the swaying men through narrow windows leaded with geometric designs. Rows of pillars linked to each other by intersecting arches made of white and red blocks marched across the broad synagogue. The walls were a brilliant bas-relief of abstract designs, and three-quarters up to the ceiling ran a series of inscriptions from *Tanach*, written in a script so decorative that it seemed an abstract design. The synagogue's ceiling was clustered with intricate geometric forms. (This synagogue was so splendid that in the middle of the thirteenth century, when Cordoba would come under Christian rule, the Pope would order an end to all renovations on it lest it outshine the Gothic and Byzantine churches.)

By the time the men stepped into the street after *Maariv*, dusk had fallen. A soft breeze blew the scent of jasmine from a nearby garden.

"My dear friend, there is a worried look upon your face," Tzadiki told Rabbi Maimon, taking hold of his arm. "You need a companion with whom you can talk."

Rabbi Maimon threw Tzadiki a curious look.

"What is it?" Tzadiki soothed him. "Come to my house, and we shall recline at my table."

A worker with a pale complexion and slanted eyes—a Russian slave—passed the two men and lit a street lamp with his torch.

"I have had a most disturbing dream," Rabbi Maimon said as they walked through the walled Jewish quarter, in which most Jews chose to live.

"A dream?" Yitzchak Tzadiki laughed. "Surely you are not letting a dream disturb you!"

"It was no ordinary dream, Yitzchak."

They passed vendors, some still crying their wares, others closing their shops. One Jew was selling fruits and vegetables; another oil, honey and spices. A butcher sluiced the street before his shop, and Rabbi Maimon and Yitzchak Tzadiki stepped about the water that coursed down the drainage depression in the middle of the street.

"And what was this dream that brought you to Cordoba?"

A veiled woman walked past them, carrying two dishes of roasted meat that she had just bought. At the corner of the street, servants were hurrying in and out of a bakery, to which they brought their own dough to bake.

"It wasn't one dream," said Rabbi Maimon. "It repeated itself, over and over again. But please, let us not discuss it here."

"I understand." Yitzchak Tzadiki patted Rabbi Maimon's arm.

The houses they passed were featureless, with the exception of a band of glazed tiles at their base and a few, high windows. Not even the gateways offered a glimpse of the dwelling within, for they opened up onto a curving path.

"This way!" Yitzchak Tzadiki led Rabbi Maimon onto a narrow street off the main road. This was little more than a winding path, already dark under the cobalt sky.

They came to a vast door.

"Hello!" Tzadiki called out.

A moment later, an adolescent servant opened the door. As Yitzchak Tzadiki unwound his headscarf, the servant disappeared and returned some moments later with an oil lamp. He led the men through a passageway to a large courtyard. In the middle of the patio was a low, square fountain with bright blue ceramics, from which they heard cascading water. About the fountain were clustered tropical shrubs, and a stone carving of a palm tree with birds. Large windows opened onto the patio.

"Very handsome!" said Rabbi Maimon.

Yitzchak Tzadiki was pleased. "We have the water piped in from the Guadalquivir."

A woman stepped into the courtyard. She wore a long dress of Spanish silk, colored a pale green. "Oh!" She exclaimed in surprise. "You have company!"

"Yocheved, tell the maid to prepare dinner for my honored guest and me."

"Certainly." She stepped back into the house.

Yitzchak Tzadiki took Rabbi Maimon's arm. "Let us go in and talk." He led Rabbi Maimon under the dusky branches of an almond and cinnamon tree and into his house.

The room that they walked into was lit by many tapers. A number of settees covered with crimson silk were scattered across the floor. *Sefarim* rested proudly in a wall niche, and a finely tooled wooden chest stood in the corner of the room.

Yitzchak Tzadiki sat down on one of the settees and crossed his legs. Rabbi Maimon sat down opposite him.

The servant brought them a tray of figs, oranges and almonds. After the two men ate of these, the servant brought in a pot filled with rice, vegetables and lamb meat. Next to it, he put down a platter that held round loaves of bread.

Yitzchak Tzadiki went to the wall and pulled aside a curtain to reveal a faucet above a glazed china basin, with a glazed ewer for washing the hands. Rabbi Maimon was astonished—running water in the house! He'd had no idea that his old friend had become so wealthy.

After the two men finished their meal, Rabbi Maimon

began to speak more freely.

"You know that I spend my days learning with Rabbi Yosef ibn Migash. What I have never told you is that I have not married until now because of my great dedication to learning Torah.

"A few weeks ago, however, I had a strange dream. An old man came to me and told me, 'There is a butcher named Shemtov in a town outside of Cordoba. Go there and marry his daughter.'

"When I awoke, I was astonished at how real the dream had seemed. But as the day wore on, I dismissed it. I am after all not a superstitious peasant. I am the seventh in a long line of *talmidei chachamim* and *dayanim*.

"But the next evening, I had the same dream, and the evening after that. Every night the same man confronts me: 'Go to the butcher Shemtov in the town outside Cordoba and marry his daughter.'

"And so," concluded Rabbi Maimon with an embarrassed smile, "I plan to go tomorrow and ask to see this Shemtov."

The servant entered. "Sir, your guests have arrived."

"Tell them that I will be with them presently," Rabbi Yitzchak said. "And make up the bed for Rabbi Maimon."

The servant withdrew to the end of the room, where he pulled a folded mattress from a large, curtained niche in the wall and began to arrange it upon the floor. "You must excuse me, Rabbi Maimon. I have to entertain some friends of mine—business acquaintances. I know that you are not a man for parties. In this room, you will find an adequate library of *sefarim*. I am sure you wish to return to your learning." Yitzchak Tzadiki got up. "Good evening."

The next morning, Rabbi Maimon followed the serpentine streets that led him to the synagogue.

After the morning prayers, he made his way to the other side of town.

Although it was early morning, the marketplace was bustling. The *kaisariya* gates were unlocked, and dealers in costly fabrics, furs, jewelry and perfumed oils were opening their shops.

As Rabbi Maimon walked out of the city gates, the countryside lay before him under a brilliant sky. An old Roman aqueduct restored by the Muslims ran alongside the fields, bringing water to farmers for tens of miles. The country was a patchwork of vineyards and orchards, with traditional fruits such as olives, as well as new fruits that the Muslims had introduced, such as oranges, lemons and apricots.

At a crossroads, Rabbi Maimon shuddered. Impaled on a tall pole as a warning to others glared the sightless head of a robber.

Toward midday, Rabbi Maimon came to the village that the old man had named in his dream. Peasants crowded about him, curious to see the Jew in rabbinic dress.

"Is there a butcher here named Shemtov?" Rabbi Maimon asked.

"Yes," the peasants and boys answered eagerly. "Down the road."

Followed by the crowd, Rabbi Maimon walked down the dusty road to a dead end.

The boys yelled out, "Shemtov! A rabbi is here to see you!"

Next to the house was a shaded courtyard where sides of beef were hung up on hooks, over which buzzed swarms of flies. A man came out from behind the house. His apron was stained with blood and as he walked forward, he rubbed his fingers on the apron, a frown on his face. "Yes, what is it?" When he saw the distinguished-looking rabbi his expression changed. "What can I do for you, rabbi?"

Rabbi Maimon cleared his throat. "Perhaps we can go indoors and speak privately."

"Of course," the butcher said. He ushered Rabbi Maimon

into the house and shut the door on the onlookers.

"Excuse me a moment." The butcher went into the back. Rabbi Maimon heard the splash of water as the butcher washed his hands. The butcher returned to the room, his hands clean and his smock replaced by a clean robe.

He sat down on a low sofa, and Rabbi Maimon did the same.

A servant brought in a tray with wine, cake and orange slices. Setting it down before the two men, he withdrew.

"Now," the butcher said, "what can I do for the noble rabbi?"

"Please tell me, do you have a daughter of marriageable age?"

"Yes, I do."

Rabbi Maimon stroked his beard. "I would like to tell you about a remarkable dream I have been having . . ." In a few sentences, he told Shemtov of the old man who had appeared to him in a dream and told him to come to this village and marry the daughter of the butcher.

For a long while, the two men sat in silence. Finally, Shemtov said, "As I understand it, you, most noble rabbi, are proposing to marry my daughter."

"Such a marriage seems to be the Will of Heaven."

"Very well! I would be honored to have you as my son-in-law. Your proposal is accepted."

A year passed. Rabbi Maimon now lived in Cordoba with his wife.

It was a *Shabbos* morning.

Through the high, square window of the synagogue, a patch of sky shone with intense blueness. A cool spring breeze blew through the chamber.

A hundred men stood on mats in the shadowy room. They swayed back and forth, chanting along with the prayer leader.

THE RAMBAM

"Yisgadal veyiskadesh Shemei Rabba . . . !"

Rabbi Maimon ben Yosef stood and listened intently to the mourner reciting the *Kaddish. "Yehei Shemei rabbah mevorach lealam ul'ulmei almaya . . . !"* The congregation repeated his words, and their voices echoed off the arched columns that receded into the shadows.

Rabbi Maimon wrapped his robe about him and stepped to the synagogue entrance to put on his shoes. Outside, the bright, lemon sunshine was streaking the whitewashed buildings across the narrow street, and the cool wind ruffled his beard.

"A good *Shabbos*, Rabbi Maimon, may your light shine!" one of the worshippers greeted him.

"Good *Shabbos*, may your end be fortunate."

Rabbi Maimon pulled his robe more tightly about him and set off briskly. He passed under an arch that linked two houses above the road and momentarily swept a shadow over him.

Thousands of Jews were spilling out of the many synagogues across the city.

For the Muslims, it was an ordinary day. Merchants were leading donkeys carrying grains, beans, seeds and brazilwood. Shopkeepers were laying out their wares: tunics, veils, turbans and kerchiefs dyed sumac-red, lilac and pistachio. In the alley sat tailors, beltmakers, coppersmiths, potter and armorers.

The Jews walked home from the synagogue seeking the quietest path through the residential streets where tucked away were little squares with fountains shaded by vine-arbors.

Rabbi Maimon hurried home.

When he had gotten up before dawn, he had leaned forward to push aside the curtain that concealed his bed in its raised alcove. In the dim light, he saw that his wife was not in the room. His maid-servant must have heard him washing his

21

hands in the bowl alongside his bed, for when he stepped out of the room, she was standing there.

"Well?"

"Your wife is all right," the wrinkled woman said. "She requests that you go to the synagogue."

In the adjoining room, Rabbi Maimon's wife sat on a low, brocaded divan. In the dim light, her eyes were shining. "It is all right. Go to synagogue and say a *Mi Shebeirach* for me."

Now Rabbi Maimon hurried home. He opened the door to a small patio paved with marble, where vines on a trellis were putting out their first leaves.

The maidservant bustled out to meet him.

"Has my wife . . . ?"

There was a cry from the other room.

"My—" He stepped forward.

"The midwife is with her. It's all right."

Rabbi Maimon stepped into the side room. Settees were placed about a carpet on which were set a large, glazed bowl filled with roasted lamb and cucumbers, and small bowls beside it. A large vase with arabesques was filled with wine, and next to it stood a *Kiddush* cup. To their side was a linen cloth inside of which were wrapped two loaves of *challah*. One had to be careful with the leaven, for tonight would begin the holiday of *Pesach*.

Rabbi Maimon sat down on the settee before the wine. Again, he heard a cry from the other room.

He got up and walked onto the patio.

A friend came onto the patio: Rabbi Tzemach, a fellow judge.

Rabbi Tzemach pulled Rabbi Maimon down to a settee. Pouring the wine for Rabbi Maimon, he put the filigreed cup into his hand.

The two men reclined at their bowls, and Rabbi Tzemach spoke cheerfully and easily. The maidservant who served them kept disappearing to take care of her mistress.

"Today is *Shabbos*!" insisted Rabbi Tzemach, and he sang a *zemer*. "Sing along with me!"

Finally, the meal was over. Rabbi Tzemach said that he would stay, but Rabbi Maimon insisted that he return to his own family.

Rabbi Maimon sat down and began reciting *Tehillim*. He had reached Chapter 81 for the second time when the silence was broken by the feeble wail of an infant.

Rabbi Maimon stood up. The maidservant came in again, her almond eyes sharp and shining and her hands clasped together. "*Mazal tov, baruch Hashem Yisbarach!*"

"Is it . . . ?"

"Come, Rabbi Maimon, come see your son!"

Rabbi Maimon followed the maid-servant into the curtained room where his wife lay on a divan tightly holding the tiny infant.

Rabbi Maimon looked down at his wife and child tenderly. The newborn infant in her arms had a wrinkled, fuzzy skull, a small, squashed face, impossibly tiny fingers and toes. He was beautiful!

The baby had been born on a *Shabbos* afternoon, *Erev Pesach*, 4895 (March 30, 1135). Little did his parents know it at the time, but the birth of this child was a turning point in Jewish history.

But for the moment, however, crisis gripped the household of Rabbi Maimon. For hours, his wife Rivkah hovered between life and death. At last, the struggle came to an end.

The doctor came out to the room where Rabbi Maimon stood, rocking his tiny baby in his arms. He looked at the doctor.

"Your wife—"

"Yes?"

"She is no longer in pain."

"Thank Heaven!" But as he saw the doctor's expression, Rabbi Maimon's look of relief changed to despair. "Is it . . . ?"

"*Baruch Dayan Emes*," said the doctor. He stepped forward to lift the child from Rabbi Maimon's slack hands.

2

Childhood

(The following story also appears in Seder Hadoros.)

Rabbi Maimon was now *dayan* and *rosh beis din* of Cordoba. After the death of his first wife in childbirth, he had married again and fathered more children.

Rabbi Maimon had great joy in his children by his second wife. They were studious and quick. But his firstborn son, whom he had named Moshe, was a trial to him. Although Moshe was already six years old, he had difficulty understanding anything he learned, and in fact, he preferred not to learn at all.

One day, Rabbi Maimon and his son were sitting together, and Moshe, as usual, was squirming.

Moshe's eyes roved over the walls. He looked out the window, and a cloud caught his attention.

"Moshe!"

Moshe looked back down into the book before him and put a stubby finger on the line. He stared blankly at the manuscript.

"You just don't want to learn, Moshe!" Rabbi Maimon exclaimed. "To think that in a family that goes back to Rabbi Yehudah Hanasi and David Hamelech, things should have come to this! A boy who would rather be out playing than learning Torah!"

Tears seeped from Moshe's eyes. "Father, I'm sorry!"

Rabbi Maimon pushed himself up from the settee in exasperation.

Moshe sprang up. His face red and his head down, he ran out of the room. Rabbi Maimon returned to his place. Picking up a *Gemara*, he began to learn.

Moshe ran to the chief synagogue of Cordoba. There he sat in a far corner, in the shadow cast by a pillar. When the congregation came in for *Minchah* and *Maariv*, no one noticed the small child, his head sagging, sobbing silently.

Late in the evening, the *shiurim* came to an end. A servant strode through the long expanse of the synagogue, putting out the oil lamps. The sandals of the last men in the synagogue slapped across the stone floor. Then the door was shut with a final bang, and the heavy lock was turned.

But Moshe heard none of these things. Long before, the weary child had fallen fast asleep. He woke up in the darkness of the cavernous synagogue, and sparks of red and gold danced before his eyes. If only he could learn Torah! A profound yearning filled his heart, and he again fell into an intense slumber.

When Moshe awoke again, thin light was filtering through the synagogue, so that the pillars looked like a ghostly forest. Distantly, he heard the chanting of the early *minyan*. Moshe lifted his head from the rug where he had lain insensibly through the night. As he struggled to his feet, a tentative joy filled his heart.

Moshe went to wash his hands at the back of the synagogue. As he passed the water over his eyes, all the Torah that he had struggled to learn sprang into his mind. Moshe's mind became sharp and broad.

Joyfully, he made his way to the *minyan* and joined the prayers. Afterwards, he picked up a *sefer* and studied a page, not sure whether this incredible gift would remain with him. To his astonishment and joy, it did. Even after he closed his eyes, he could see the words as though he were still reading from the book. G-d had performed a miracle!

Moshe imagined how he would go home and show this to his father.

As Moshe prepared to leave, he heard his father's voice. At the other side of the synagogue, Rabbi Maimon held close to him David, one of his children from his new wife.

Tears came to Moshe's eyes, and he bit his lower lip to keep from crying. No! he thought. He would not try to win his father's love.

Instead, he would go off and learn Torah only because he wanted to. He slipped to the far side of the synagogue and left.

Moshe hurried down the broad, sunny street. In one alley, where confectioneries were being sold, Moshe bought a small cake for breakfast with his last few coins.

As though mirroring his inner clarity, the day was crisp, bright and clear. Approaching the gate of the city, Moshe came to a decision. He would leave Cordoba altogether and travel southward to Lucena, where he would learn under Rabbi Yosef ibn Migash, the great teacher from whom his own father had learned.

Moshe was a charming boy, and he soon got a lift with a cloth merchant travelling as far as Aguilar. Their wagon rolled slowly through vine and olive groves, sometimes dipping into valleys filled with wild scrub and rising up rocky hillsides where peasants had terraced the land into a thousand tiny orchards of lime and avocado trees.

After seeing to Moshe's care, the merchant arranged a place for him to stay overnight. Early the next morning, Moshe was awakened by the merchant, next to whom stood another Jew. "Young man, get up and say your prayers quickly. This horse dealer has agreed to take you to Lucena."

Soon Moshe was again riding in a carriage. Three hours later, the scattered farmhouses on the green plains began to cluster together, and the walls of Lucena appeared in the distance.

The *yeshivah* of Rabbi Yosef ibn Migash was the greatest Torah academy in all of Spain. It had been founded a generation before by the teacher of Rabbi ibn Migash, Rabbi Yitzchak Alfasi (famous for his *halachic* condensation of the *Gemara*, *Hilchos Rav Alfasi*, the Rif).

A few days afterward, Moshe stood in the courtyard of the *yeshivah* as a tiled fountain trickled water amidst three palm trees. A student in his mid-teens with wisps of hair on his cheeks was speaking to the boy. "I am surprised that the *rosh yeshivah* allowed you in to learn. Usually, a child your age would be sent back home."

Moshe had not revealed that he was the son of the famous Rabbi Maimon.

Rabbi Yosef ibn Migash was very devoted to Moshe, and told his other students, "My sons, know that this young one will be a great man, and all of Israel, from east to west, will walk in his light." (*Divrei Hayamim* of Rabbi Saadia ibn Danon, published in *Sefer Chemdah Genuzah*, and quoted in *Harambam*, by N. T. Sifrai) Moshe remained with Rabbi Yosef ibn Migash for a short while, quickly becoming an outstanding child prodigy.

A few months after Moshe came to Lucena, Rabbi Yosef

ibn Migash died in *Iyar* of 4901 (1141).

The Chida tells that "before the death of the Ri Migash, young Moshe came to his deathbed and kissed his hands. The Ri Migash bestirred himself and blessed him before his soul left him." (*Shem Hagedolim*)

It was said later that with this kiss, the wisdom of the Ri Migash came to rest upon the Rambam.

Moshe took leave of the other students and returned to Cordoba.

But even now, he did not go home.

On *Shabbos*, Moshe went to the main synagogue and sat in an inconspicuous corner.

After the reading of the Torah, Moshe stepped onto the *bimah*. His head was barely higher than the railing.

"Who is that boy?"

"Rabbi Maimon! That's your son who ran away!"

Moshe raised his voice above the clamor and began to expound the Torah.

He spoke wondrous words of wisdom. Even if they had been spoken by an adult, they would have been sweeter than the honeycomb. And to hear such brilliance, maturity and knowledge on the lips of a small child!

When Moshe finished speaking, his father came up to him, young David at his side. "Welcome home," Rabbi Maimon said. He took Moshe by the shoulders and kissed him, and Moshe felt his father's tear brush against his cheek.

3

Into Exile

THE RAMBAM WAS RAISED IN AN ATMOSPHERE OF CULTURE AND
intellectual excitement.

Cordoba was a cosmopolitan center of Jewish life. In the
midst of a brilliant Muslim civilization, Jews blended dedication to Torah with intellectual interest in all the arts and
sciences.

In the tenth century, Chisdai ibn Shaprut, the great
statesman and supporter of Torah, had lived in Cordoba.
Some years later, the *talmid chacham*, poet and statesman
Rabbi Shmuel Hanagid spent his youth in Cordoba. Then,
some years before the birth of the Rambam, Rabbi Yehudah
Halevi learned in Cordoba's famous *yeshivah*. Here he won a
popular poetry-composing contest held among Jews, in em-
ulation of Arab practice.

Jews had lived in Cordoba for over a thousand years. There

were many wealthy dynasties whose members were both conversant with the culture about them and loyal to the Torah.

It was a gray, chill day. The streets were damp from the morning rain, and the sky was a solid mass of dirty smoky clouds. In the *beis midrash*, Moshe sat among a group of young men on low stools, their feet folded on the gold and black rug. Before them sat Rabbi Maimon, teaching from a *Gemara*.

In the late afternoon, Rabbi Maimon and his young son walked home together. Although the sky had cleared, a strong, wet wind still gusted through the streets. Passersby hurried, their brightly-dyed robes flapping about them.

A hundred miles to the south, watchtowers on the coast flashed messages of alarm in a chain from Gibraltar to the north.

A soldier in Gibraltar scrawled a message on a dozen scraps of parchment. Climbing a steep ladder to a flat roof, he stepped to a dovecote. Down in the street, three of his comrades lay bloody, and an invader on horseback trampled one of the bodies. With trembling fingers, the soldier caught the fluttering birds one by one and tied the messages to their feet.

He heard a shout.

"Up there, men! One of their soldiers is with the carrier pigeons. Get him!"

The soldier opened the door and waved his arms at the pigeons. "Get out!"

Two foreign soldiers climbed the ladder onto the roof and rushed at the soldier with their short, curved swords.

As the soldier fell on his back with a cry of pain and horror, he saw the pigeons flashing into the sky, carrying his message to the military outposts of the coast and north.

Black slaves also were running to bring the disastrous news of the invasion to the many caliphs of Muslim Spain.

In Rabbi Maimon's house, the servant had already lit the candles. "Rabbi Yosef ibn Tzaddik is awaiting you in the reception room."

"Thank you, Guzman." Although a religious Jew, the servant, like many other Jews of Muslim Spain, only had an Arabic name.

With a smile, Rabbi Maimon strode into the next room.

There was a whisper: "Moshe!"

Moshe turned to see his brother David. "Come on," he whispered back. "Father is going to discuss Torah with Rabbi ibn Tzaddik!"

The two boys entered the reception room after their father.

Rabbi Yosef ibn Tzaddik rose from a settee, helping himself up with one hand, holding a bound *sefer* in the other. He was tall and thin, his hair white. "Rabbi Maimon, I hope you do not mind. I have been looking at your book of *halachos* on prayer and the holidays." Rabbi Yosef ibn Tzaddik shook the manuscript. "Perhaps it should be translated into Hebrew for our brothers in the Christian lands who do not understand Arabic."

"Rabbi Yosef, you are too generous. It is your *Olam Katan* that deserves to be spread among all the communities of Israel."

Rabbi Yosef ibn Tzaddik was a *dayan* who served on the same *beis din* as did Rabbi Maimon. He was deeply engaged in philosophic inquiry and developed his ideas in *Olam Katan*, a work that rested upon the idea of man as a microcosm of the universe.

More guests came. Moshe remained in the room, listening intently to every discussion.

Here two *talmidei chachamim* were discussing what

they had learned as students of the Ri Migash. In another corner of the room, a number of men were reciting by heart the poetry of Rabbi Yehudah Halevi.

Three men reclining before a dish of rice and roast lamb were talking about Avraham ibn Ezra. Seven years before, in 1135, he had fled an uprising in Tudela and come to Rome.

"I hear that he has begun writing a commentary on *Tanach*. Is that true?"

A man with a pointed beard put a cherry in his mouth. "I know that he wrote a commentary on *Koheles*. But I don't know if . . ."

Moshe listened to the *talmidei chachamim* discussing the philosophical views of Rabbi Shlomo ibn Gabirol in his *Mekor Chaim* and the path of serving G-d that Rabbi Bachya ibn Pakudah had set out in his *Hidaya ila Fara'id al-kulub (Chovos Halevovos)*.

The comforts of the food, the beauty of the architecture, the quiet, measured speech in Arabic, the company of the leaders of the Jews of Cordoba, all of them well-to-do and of honored families, sent a spirit of gladness over the evening.

Servants passed among the men with wine and sweet apricots, and two censers blew the scent of jasmine into the air.

Young Moshe absorbed the spirit and knowledge of this environment. He viewed with reverence all the *talmidei chachamim* and especially his own father and his father's tradition.

Rabbi Maimon was talking with some colleagues about the great Torah tradition of Spain. There was a brief lull in the room, and Moshe's young voice broke the silence. "Father, how long have Jews lived in Cordoba?"

"Are you still awake, Moshe?" Rabbi Maimon asked brusquely, but his eyes were laughing. "Come here. There is a tradition that our forefathers came to Spain during the time of the destruction of the first Beis Hamikdash, over seventeen hundred years ago. Nevuchadnezzar conquered Yerushalayim together with King Aspian. They divided the spoils and the Jews among themselves. Aspian received the section of Jerusalem where the leaders of the Jews and the offspring of the house of David Hamelech lived. These Jews were taken to Spain, which is named after King Aspian.

"We are the offspring of those Jews. So you can see that we have been here in Cordoba a very long time—"

Meanwhile, the watchtowers had been signalling to each other up the coast from Gibraltar.

The black messenger slaves had entered the cities of Ios Gazules, Jimena and Los Barrios. And the carrier pigeons had flown to Cortes, Ronda, Puenta Genil—and to Cordoba.

There was a staccato knock at the door. The servant opened the door to one of Rabbi ibn Tzaddik's students, who was panting heavily. "Please let me in. I have an important message to deliver."

The student entered the room and halted at the doorway. Catching sight of his teacher talking to Rabbi Maimon, he strode up to them.

"Excuse me for interrupting," the student said. "We just received word that the Almohads have invaded Gibraltar."

Since 1086, Muslim Spain had been under the control of a faction of Muslims called Ummayads.

In the 1120s, a Berber from Morocco named Mohammed ibn Tumrat began a movement that became known as the Almohads—"believers in the oneness of G-d."

In 1139, when Tumrat died, his disciple, Abd Almumin, took control.

Abd Almumin began a holy war and within a year conquered North Africa, including Morocco. Here he began immediately to persecute Christians and Jews.

It is told that Abd Almumin gathered the Jewish leaders of

Morocco together and told them, "You are waiting for the messiah, but we know that he was supposed to come five hundred years after the death of Mohammed. Since he hasn't done so, you now have the choice of conversion or death."

After much pleading, the Jews persuaded him to allow them to leave Morocco.

Abd Almumin now turned his sights to Spain. It was his intent to cast out the worldly, spoiled leaders of Muslim Spain's city-states and absorb them in a unified empire.

Moshe ben Maimon was seven years old when Abd Almumin invaded Spain.

In Cordoba, the life of the established community continued as before.

Cordoba's *yeshivah*, the foremost *yeshivah* on the Iberian Peninsula, was still crowded with students who learned Talmud. Every week, Jewish fund collectors gathered taxes for the Jewish hospitals, orphanages and an educational system that went from kindergarten through high school.

Jewish craftsmen still turned out rare leatherwork; thirteen thousand Jewish weavers still sat at their looms, creating wool and cotton fabrics that were sold all across Europe.

Farmers still led donkeys laden with overflowing bags of fruit, grain and vegetables. The marketplaces were still filled with the rich scents of perfumes and the sound of traders speaking a dozen languages.

But Moshe could no longer feel that life was safe.

The students from North Africa could not go home. What had happened to their families? Some had fled. Others had pretended to convert or had actually converted; and others had been killed.

And in Spain, the Almohads had conquered Málaga, Granada and Lucena, destroying the synagogues and *yeshivos* that had stood for hundreds of years, converting some of them into mosques (they did the same to the churches).

Wherever they entered, they gave the Jews (as well as the Christians) three choices: convert to Islam, go into exile or die.

Thousands of refugees streamed into Cordoba. Farmers and makers of goods for export could no longer rely on the usual routes of trade; food and other goods became scarcer.

A few months after the invasion of Spain, Rabbi Maimon's close friend, Rabbi Yosef ibn Tzadok, died.

There was less to rely on, more fear, more uncertainty.

Abd Almumin's invasion aroused Muslims in Cordoba to greater strictness. When Moshe walked to the *yeshivah*, he heard speakers on the street exhorting Muslims to stop their wine-drinking parties.

One morning, Moshe saw a crowd of Muslims standing before a tall speaker in a thick, red turban, gesturing vigorously with his fist.

" . . . too long have we suffered the *dhimmis*—the Jews and Christians—to be like us. Fellow Muslims, keep the Koran faithfully, and cast the *dhimmi* down from the position that you have allowed him to attain."

The speaker reached into his robe and pulled out a sheet. "Listen to the dictates of Islam:

"No *dhimmi* may build a synagogue or church in addition to any that had existed before the faith of Islam.

"No *dhimmi* may hire a Muslim.

"A *dhimmi* must stand in the presence of a Muslim.

"A *dhimmi* must house a Muslim traveller for three days.

"No *dhimmi* may prevent any other *dhimmi* from converting to Islam.

"No *dhimmi* may dress or wear his hair in such a manner that he may be mistaken for a Muslim. No *dhimmi* may wear silk belts or shoes of colors worn by Muslims.

"No *dhimmi* may have a Muslim name.

"In the bathhouse, a *dhimmi* man must wear a special sign

about his neck. *Dhimmi* women may not bathe in the same bathhouses used by Muslim women.

"No *dhimmi* may be allowed to ride on a horse or mule—only on a jackass.

"No *dhimmi* may use a riding saddle. He must sit side-saddle on a pack saddle with no ornamentation.

"No *dhimmi* house may be higher than a Muslim house. No *dhimmi* tomb may be higher than a Muslim tomb.

"No *dhimmi* may be employed by the government or have any position giving him authority over any Muslim."

The preacher waved the parchment in his hand.

"The Koran commands us to treat the Jew and Christian as second-class citizens. So why do Jewish merchants hire Muslims? Why are Jews more honored than us in our universities, marketplaces and residences? Why do we see Jews as physicians and government officials?

"Brothers! Everything about the appearance of a *dhimmi* must proclaim his degradation and the honor of the Muslim. The appearance of a *dhimmi* must be a witness and a testimony . . . "

Moshe slunk away from the crowd of men.

A new type of Muslim—stupid, ignorant and destructive—was taking over. Who would have dreamed that such brutish men with crude appeals to mass prejudice could exist, much less gain large followings?

The Ummayad Muslims, too, felt the destruction of their civilization. The poet, ibn Baqi, lamented,

> *"The rhymes of poetry weep their fill*
> *For an Arab lost among barbarians."*

No longer were the marketplace stalls overflowing with luxuries. No longer did the youthful dandies parade down the street with the calves of their legs gilded.

Still, Moshe learned Torah as well as the sciences from his father and in close comradeship with his beloved brother—David.

In 1148, Moshe became *bar-mitzvah*.

Two months later, the Almohads invaded Cordoba.

Soldiers ran down the streets trampling men in their way, overturning market stalls and barrels of wine.

Breaking into the synagogues, they ripped down *sifrei Torah* and captured rabbis and wealthy merchants.

There was no longer bread. Family members were separated from one another. Men, women and children were maimed and murdered by the marauding soldiers.

In *Sefer Hakabbalah*, the Raavad reported, "The years following the death of Rabbi Yosef Halevi (the Ri Migash) were years of destruction and trouble for the Jews. They were forced into wandering. Some died, some were killed, some starved and some were taken prisoner. In 4902 (1142), the Almohads decreed forced apostasy against the Jews in order to destroy us, and left nothing . . . "

Rabbi Avraham ibn Ezra mourned the destruction:

"Great evil has descended on Spain from heaven
And deep mourning on North Africa.
Our hands are weakened and our eyes are filled with tears.
I weep when I gaze upon the city of Lucena.
Although it was not guilty the exile took root there.
It was a city that was, without exaggeration, a thousand and
seventy years old.
And now this day arrived:
The people left, and the city was widowed,
Without Torah, without Tanach; the mishneh was hidden
And the Talmud abandoned, for all its glory left it.
Some people were killed, and others sought refuge.
The synagogues were turned into mosques—
And a strange, cruel nation has called itself the true religion!

I will weep and strike my hands in mourning, and I will wail.
I cannot be still; I am overcome with grief.
I tear out my hair and I bitterly cry for the exile of Seville,
For the leaders and wise men, the lords who were murdered,
For their children taken captive, for their daughters and
pampered women forced to convert.
How abandoned is Cordoba, like a stormy sea.
In Almidia, not one Jew remains.
In Morocco and Málaga, there is no food.
The Jews have been injured and dealt a terrible blow.
I will cry out, I will speak bitterly, I will sigh and groan,
I will wail in deepest sadness."

The houses of marble, the long, irrigated fields, the mosaics of porphyry and jasper, the splendidly saddled horses standing before the homes of the wealthy—all these were destroyed by the Almohads.

Jews had to wear yellow clothes, and Christians blue. They also had to wear a special belt, called a *zunnar*. In addition, the turban worn by *dhimmi*s had to have different color or shape than that worn by the Muslim.

Almumin's commanders now circulated among the Jews and Christians with the Almohad ultimatum. "All *dhimmi*s must convert to Islam, lose their lives or leave the areas under Almohad rule."

Moshe was witness to the distressed Jews who came to Rabbi Maimon.

One meeting was lasting late into the night.

"This is the end of Cordoba!" one Jew was saying. "It was a sweet exile. But now we must leave everything behind and seek another country that will take us in."

"Enough wandering!" interrupted a young man with a ginger beard. "Why should we live upon the unclean land of the nations? Let us return to our holy land and plow our own ground."

Another man moved his head back and clicked his tongue. "Please, Reb Ovadiah! We are here to come up with a practical solution. It is obvious that we have to leave Cordoba. But the question is: where to?"

A man in a black, woollen robe stood up with an irritated expression. "Why do we assume that we must leave Cordoba? Gentlemen, Jews have lived here a thousand years. The invasion of this Almohad is barely worth considering. His time will pass in the twinkling of an eye."

"But he threatens us with death!" a voice called out.

"Please!" the man in the black robe replied. "Have we Jews not been threatened with death before? Have we not survived the Babylonians, the Romans and the Greeks? We must consider our investment in Cordoba: a thousand years of building our community. Gentlemen, I appeal to you. We can hardly contemplate uprooting the religious infrastructure we have created: Our *yeshivos*, our synagogues and our *mikvaos*."

"But the Almohads threaten to kill us!" the same voice replied.

The man in the black robe put up his hand. "Then we must deal with the problem instead of running away from it. Our question must be: What steps can we take to thwart the haters and promote an atmosphere of security in our neighborhoods?"

The discussion lasted for hours. Finally, Rabbi Maimon declared, "Gentlemen, there is no question that we cannot continue to live in Cordoba. I and my family will become wanderers upon the road. Let us thank G-d that at least we have been offered the choice of leaving."

In the week that followed, almost the entire Jewish population streamed out of Cordoba. Families left behind their houses, farms and businesses. It was difficult to sell anything at a fair price, because the Arabs knew that the Jews had no choice.

Most Jews fled to the north, where the clement Alfonso ruled over Christian Spain. Alfonso offered these Jews refuge in the capital city of Tudela. In gratitude, many Jews joined his army to fight the Almohads.

Other Jews travelled further north across the Pyrenees to Provence.

Still other Jews travelled westward to Portugal. Among them were the son and nephew of Rabbi Yosef ibn Migash, both called Rabbi Meir. The two of them opened a *yeshivah* there. A Jewish minister in the Portuguese government, Don Yichiah, made it easy for the Jews to immigrate.

Some Jews travelled over sea and land to Egypt.

Almost every Jewish community in Muslim Spain was destroyed. Tens of thousands of Jews were on the roads.

Only a handful of Jews remained in Cordoba. Some could not leave because of old age, or because of a beloved family member. Challenged by the Almohad rulers to declare their conversion to Islam, some refused and were put to death. Others declared themselves to be Muslim, while privately loyal to the Torah. And other Jews managed to avoid making such a vow. They pretended to be Muslim and kept the Torah in private.

These secret Jews lived in constant fear of exposure. The penalty for allegiance to the Torah was death, and many died. Some secret Jews managed to keep their Jewishness alive for many generations. Sometimes the children would know only that they kept a strange custom, such as lighting candles Friday night.

It was a hot, dry morning when Rabbi Maimon and his family set out from Cordoba amidst a stream of refugees. Jackasses pulled the carts on which they had packed the provisions they would need on the road.

The grape vines and olive tree leaves were withering

under the hot sun. The dry dust of the road blew up in little clouds and dusted the Jews' robes.

In the fields, Arab farmers bent over the crops. They seemed as immutable as the rising and setting of the sun, as insensible of change as the hawks wheeling overhead in the blue sky.

The long row of refugees walked along the bank of the great Guadalquivir River. They were the wealthy and indigent, young and old, pious and secularized, sophisticated and simple.

Sometimes the road they walked on spanned an irrigation canal through which ran brown, sediment-filled water. Looking at the broad landscape, Moshe saw the many draw-wells, cisterns and ditches that had been dug into the countryside to make the region of Cordoba so fertile.

Some of the larger canals were fed water by waterwheels as large as houses. Moshe passed within twenty feet of such a wheel. It had scoops that caught the water. As the river turned the wheel, the scoops carried the water high up and spilled it into a canal.

Looking ahead, Moshe saw a line of great waterwheels fading into the horizon, bringing fecundity to the countryside and its inhabitants.

As for the Jews, all that remained to them was their allegiance to the words of Torah, which are compared to water. "Blessed is the man who trusts in Hashem so that Hashem is his trust; he is like a tree planted upon the water, sending out its roots upon the water channel." (*Yirmiyahu* 17:7-8)

Rabbi Maimon decided not to travel northward. He travelled instead to the Christian-held port city of Almería, one hundred and thirty miles southwest of Cordoba—a six days' journey.

Almohad and Ummayad soldiers roamed the roads, and

passing Jews told stories of blood and grieving. It was the season of heat and dust, and thousands of Jews straggled along the roads in torn clothes. Wealthy Jews led jackasses loaded with fabrics, vessels and clothing. Others concealed gems and gold in their belts or carried precious musk in vials around their necks.

From farmers along the way, Rabbi Maimon purchased food and drink. These farmers now looked at the Jews with hostility and suspicion.

In the evening, Rabbi Maimon and his family found refuge in an overcrowded hostel outside Lucena. The crush, the cries and whispers of fleeing refugees were overwhelming. Rabbi Maimon made his way up to the flat roof of the hostel, which was also crowded with refugees.

Above his head, the stars twinkled calmly. In the distance flickered glowing sheets of orange and white. Lucena, the city from which Torah had spread to all of Spanish Jewry, was being put to the flame.

Rabbi Maimon turned and climbed back down the rickety ladder to his wife and children.

The family travelled westward past Montefrío and turned south along the Almería River to Almería.

Here the Maimons settled. While the Almohads created exile and upheaval, Rabbi Maimon and Moshe devoted their days and nights to the study of Torah. Moshe's brother David was also pious and learned, and he learned together with them. But he was as well a man of action, a man of business.

Whatever Moshe learned, he remembered. And every bit of knowledge had its place in his mind. He could compare whatever he learned to all the other information in the Torah or infer from what he had learned whatever *halachos* needed to be clarified.

Like most Spanish scholars, Moshe also learned the sciences of astronomy, logic, mathematics and medicine.

Ships landed at Almería carrying merchandise from all over the world. From India came panther skins and rubies; from China, paper, cinnamon and silk; from Arabia, pedigreed camels and horses; from Barbary, hawks and salam leaves for tanning; from Yemen, giraffes; from Isfanhan, quinces and saffron.

David would walk along the bustling docks as teams of slaves, their skin glistening in the Mediterranean sun, unloaded loads of indigo, white lead, wool and cages filled with quail. He would listen to the merchants haggle, while seamen in grimy costumes clambered among the boats.

Meanwhile, Moshe's stepmother and sisters remained within their quarters, rarely venturing out. When they did go into the street, they were accompanied by their father or one of their brothers, and they wore a veil that only revealed their eyes.

For three years, Moshe and his family remained in Almería. Now, in 1151, he was sixteen years old.

During these years, the Almohads had continued spreading across Spain.

In 1151, the Almohads invaded Almería.

Soldiers galloped through the streets. As the Jews hid in their homes, they heard the cries of triumph and violent death, the smashing of shops, the crackling fires.

The next day, all the Jews were summoned to the market square.

Rabbi Maimon and his children passed by captive Ummayad soldiers tied to one another by chains on their necks. These were the ones whose fate would be merciful: they would be sold into slavery.

In the crowded square, soldiers stood at every entranceway, holding swords crusted brown with blood.

"Jews!" the army commander shouted. "We have come to bring the true law of Islam to Almería! You must convert to

Islam. Failing that, you have two choices. The first is very simple." He ran his finger across his neck, and the soldiers laughed. "The second choice is also simple." He pointed his finger and waved it in a semi-circle from left to right. "Go wherever your feet will take you."

With the other Jews of Almería, the family of Maimon were again cast into exile.

Rabbi Maimon decided to travel to another city in Christian Spain. This time, they would head north and traverse the Sierra Morena mountain range. Again they travelled from village to village, avoiding the cities, and the soldiers and marauders.

As they came to the Sierra Morena Range, the villages grew more infrequent. Now they occasionally passed a wild goat herd or a few stone houses nestled in a green valley along barren hills covered with shale and scrub.

At night, they lay down to sleep before a flickering fire. As Moshe closed his eyes, he would hear the howls of wolves. Then someone would arise and stoke the fire, and everyone would take turns standing guard in the chill darkness, as the damp branches crackled and sent up black, sparking smoke.

At last, they crossed the mountain pass and began the northern descent, passing through *maquis*—woodland about shoulder high—relieved by occasional clumps of conifers and oaks, and sometimes changing to impenetrable thickets of shrubs.

At last, Rabbi Maimon and his family arrived at a small city, with houses crowded about the walls of a Moorish castle. But they found no resting place here either.

For another seven years, they wandered from city to city and town to town, crossing the border between Christian Spain and those sections of Muslim Spain not yet under Almohad rule. It is possible that they crossed the Pyrenees and travelled as far north as Provence. Even as the Almohads fought the Ummayads, the Christians fought against the Almohads and Ummayads together. Even as the Almohads persecuted the Jews, so did the Christians.

Rabbi Moshe wrote of this period of his life, "G-d decreed upon us exile and wandering from one end of the heavens to the other when my mind was troubled, amid exiles ordained by heaven, on journeys by land and on the stormy sea." (End of *Pirush Hamishnayos*)

Wherever they went, they saw the suffering of thousands of Jews. Moshe mourned for the pain of all those that he saw: those who had lost their homes, and those who had lost their parents; those who had lost their wives and children, and those who had lost hope.

The Torah was in disarray and the wise men in exile. The *batei midrash* had been destroyed and the men of understanding scattered. The new generation was destitute and desperate. Nevertheless, wherever they went, Rabbi Maimon, Moshe and David learned Torah, for the Torah was the purpose of life. The ignorant person may prefer the consolations of this world. But the wise man knows that the way to come close to G-d is via the perfection of his intellectual faculties through the study of Torah.

Moshe was now in his late teens. He and his family had come to a small city in the north of Spain at the foothills of the Pyrenees, where the wind rushed through the mountain passes, bringing damp air and rain. The house he was sitting in, with its stone walls, shuttered windows and narrow chimney, was damp and chill.

A gangling youth walked into the room. A black sidelock crept out from under his turban and lay across his cheek.

"Rabbi Moshe!" he called out.

Rabbi Moshe looked up from the *sefer* he was studying. He smiled and pulled a thin manuscript from under the *sefer* and held it out to the young man.

"You did it already!" The young man came over and took the manuscript.

He sat off to the side and began reading it. Finally, he looked up at Rabbi Moshe. He put out his right hand, clenching his fist and holding up his thumb. "Good! Now I can at last begin to understand the *halachos* of the calendar."

A few weeks earlier, he had complained to Rabbi Moshe, "I can't make heads or tails of the discussions in the *Gemara* about the new month and how to figure out the year. If only someone could explain some astronomy to me, so that it could make some sense . . ."

Now Rabbi Moshe had written for him a booklet which is today known as *Maamar Ha'ibbur* (or *Cheshbon Ha'ibbur*)—the *Essay on Intercalation*.

In his work, Rabbi Moshe clarified the movements of the spheres of the sky, the division of the seasons and how to calculate the new moon and determine leap years.

The booklet shows the mature grasp that Rabbi Moshe had of astronomy and mathematics, as well as his talent for explaining confusing material in a lucid fashion. His purpose, he wrote, was to make it possible to learn this topic easily and without strain.

Another year arrived, and they were in another city. The spring rains had sprinkled on the broad valleys where the figs were ripening, and the peasants stooped in the glittering rice paddies.

As Rabbi Moshe had travelled with his father, he too had become known as an outstanding *talmid chacham*.

A community leader asked him to explain the foundations of logic. Rabbi Moshe wrote a small book, *Biur Milos Hahegayon—Explanation of Logical Terms*.

It is necessary to know the basic rules of logic before being able to understand the discussions of the Talmud, Rabbi Moshe said. "Logic is to intellect as grammar is to language."

But these works were merely the condiments to wisdom. Rabbi Moshe now also began writing directly on the Torah.

As Rabbi Moshe walked through the town one day, he could see the broad expanse of the valley under the May sun. The ears of wheat had already begun to form, and the fields shivered in the spring breeze. On the olive trees and grape vines, the fruit had begun to appear, and bees hovered among the flowers and tree blossoms.

Housewives were carrying baskets of nuts to preserve, and farmers guided large-shouldered oxen over the rich soil.

A Jewish family walked wearily up the dirt road and entered the town.

"*Shalom aleichem*!" Rabbi Moshe greeted the family.

"*Aleichem shalom.*" The older man wiped his hand across his face.

"Where do you come from?"

"Calatayud."

"What is the situation there?"

The older man raised his arms and shrugged his shoulders.

"Is the *yeshivah* still open?"

"*Yeshivah?*" the old man said to Rabbi Moshe angrily. "In these times, who can learn in a *yeshivah*?"

He and his family continued trudging up the hill and disappeared amidst the white-walled houses.

Rabbi Moshe gazed at the valley. The Torah was being forgotten. No one could sit in *yeshivah* and spend years learning to understand the Talmud. There was no commentary that explained the Talmud—for although Rashi had already written his commentary, it had not made its way to Muslim Spain.

Rabbi Moshe knew what his mission and ability were: he would make the Torah accessible to Jews.

Rabbi Moshe began composing a commentary on the

Talmud, covering the tractates included in the Orders of *Moed*, *Nashim* and *Nezikin*, as well as the tractate of *Chulin*, because it contains crucial information on the laws of *kashrus*. (He refers to this in his introduction to his *Pirush Hamishnayos*.)

At the same time, he composed a wide-ranging work called *Hilchos Yerushalmi*. This was analogous to the *Hilchos Habavli* of the Rif. He presented a digest of the Talmud Yerushalmi, with a stress on the *halachic* outcome.

Rabbi Moshe wrote much of the material in these works from memory because during his travels he did not have access to many *sefarim*.

Unfortunately, none of these works have survived, besides a few fragments.

Rabbi Moshe also began another endeavor, one that would endure to this day: his *Pirush Hamishnayos*.

Such a commentary had never before been attempted. Rabbi Moshe wrote in the introduction to his work, "To this day, confusion has grown in learning *mishneh*. Even if one is the greatest of *geonim*, one cannot understand a *mishneh* without first learning the entire relevant portion of the *Gemara* with its give and take. But the discussions in the *Gemara* are sometimes drawn out to four or five pages on one *halachah*, filled with argument and debate. As a result, only an expert in in-depth learning can correctly clarify the meaning of the *mishneh*."

Rabbi Moshe set out to write a conceptual, all-encompassing commentary. He would write introductions to *sedarim* and *mesechtos*, giving overviews of *halachah* and philosophy. His commentaries on the individual *mishnayos* would clarify the meaning of the text and then tell what the actual *halachah* was.

This massive work took ten years to write during ten years of wandering across the Mediterranean.

Meanwhile, in 1159, the family settled in Muslim-controlled Tudela, situated in the center of Spain.

Seder Hadoros tells that one night, Arab bandits entered the central mosque of Tudela and stole its treasures.

The next morning, when the guards discovered the theft, they were terrified that they would lose their lives. They ran to the town leaders and blamed the theft on a poor Jew named Avraham del Capa.

The Muslims were enraged. They ran through the streets of Tudela, pulling Jews from their houses and murdering them, and they broke into the synagogues and tore them apart. When the pogrom was over, forty synagogues had been destroyed. The Muslims rounded up all the Jews that they could lay their hands on and forcibly converted them.

In the rout, Rabbi Maimon and his family fled. Stumbling along a pitch-black road lit only by a sizzling torch, they walked back south. South or north, what did it matter? All Spain was in the grip of the nightmare. If they had ever had any hopes that Cordoba would again be freed, these had been shattered with the traumatic scenes that still trembled in their memories: women and children slaughtered, men dragged behind horses, *Sifrei Torah* cast into the offal.

In the dry, oppressive darkness that lay heavily upon the countryside, Rabbi Maimon said, "We have suffered long enough in Spain. May the Merciful One lead us to a land where we may rest, each man under the shade of his vine."

4

Morocco

THE SMALL *DHOW* WAS CROWDED WITH ARABS AND JEWS. SAILORS climbed the mainmast, made of a twisted tree trunk, to hoist the yardsail with coconut husk fiber cordage, and a boy bailed the bilge with a stinking goatskin bucket. Rabbi Maimon and his family sat toward the prow of the ship.

It was a short passage across the Bay of Gibraltar from Tarif, the southernmost point of Spain, to Tangier in Morocco. Toward the late afternoon, they huddled and ate unleavened bread and fish together with the *nakhoda*—the captain—a lean, bearded Yemenite. The ragged sail billowed, and spray splashed onto the passengers and their possessions.

At nightfall, the *dhow* came to port. Rabbi Maimon and his family followed a Moroccan Jew, who introduced himself as Mansour, through serpentine lanes to his home.

The men sat upon low cushions in a room separate from

the women. Mansour's wife entered with a terra cotta tray and placed it on the leather mat that served as a table.

A servant brought in a pitcher and bowl and poured water over the men's hands. Each man dipped his bread into the platter and ate from the section of the platter that lay before him. Couscous was heaped about the border of the tray, which Mansour ate by rolling a handful into a ball and popping it into his mouth so that his hand did not touch his mouth. A hollow in the center of the tray was filled with chicken stew.

After the men finished, they retired to the living room, and the women came in to eat.

"You come to Morocco at a merciful time," Mansour told Rabbi Maimon as they drank *machya* brandy. "For over a decade, we have suffered deeply under the Almohads. Many of us have been killed and many others converted under threat of death. We must pretend to be Muslim in our public life. Many Jews are weakening in their loyalty to the Torah.

"But now G-d has turned the heart of the cruel Abd Almumin, and we have begun to see some respite. Where do you intend to settle?"

"With G-d's help," Rabbi Maimon replied, "we will set out tomorrow morning for Fez."

"Of course. The great Rabbi Yehudah HaKohen ibn Shushan lives there."

"How is his situation?"

"He maintains a *yeshivah* in secret, at the risk of his life."

Soon the brass lamps were extinguished, and Rabbi Maimon and his family went to sleep.

In the marketplace the following morning, Rabbi Maimon hired three camels to carry his family and their possessions.

They set out as part of a caravan of eight merchants and a guide onto a steep road leading down to a dingy valley.

Four days later, under a sky in which wisps of long, thin clouds floated, they arrived at Fez. The wall was a splotchy dun, like the color of the surrounding dusty hills. The houses too were gray white, an expanse of buildings locked tightly together. Because almost all the windows were only open to the inner courtyards, it seemed a city of intricate, forbidding walls. Here and there was a patch of color: a minaret rising from a green-roofed mosque, a green cypress tree or a cluster of orange trees.

Along the side of the road, a shepherd in tatters sat on a rock. A black goat with small horns stood in the thick branches of an argan tree, nibbling the narrow leaves.

They entered the city gate. Built on the side of a hill, the city sloped steeply down.

Alongside their camels, Rabbi Maimon and his family walked between high, whitewashed walls, the doors of the houses painted blue for good luck.

In the midst of the city, one could not appreciate its vastness: its seven hundred and eighty-five mosques, and chapels, eighty fountains, ninety public baths, five hundred inns, one hundred thousand houses and nine thousand five hundred shops.

One of the traders who had travelled with their caravan, a hidden Jew named ibn Hassan, led the Maimons to the quarter where many hidden Jews lived.

"A pity!" ibn Hassan sighed. "According to our traditions, Jews have lived in Morocco since the time of the Tanach, when Jews came here to purchase gold and fight the Plishtim.

"Then, before the Muslims conquered the land in the 600s, entire tribes of Berbers gave up their idol worship and became Jewish.

"And who could forget the battles against the invading Muslims, when entire communities of Jews joined together with non-Jewish tribes?

"Who could ever forget the Jewish queen of the tribes, Dahiya the Prophetess, who led the battle against the invading

Muslims until she was killed in 707?

"And for the last one hundred and fifty years, we enjoyed our golden age. Everywhere there were *yeshivos*.

"But now look at us! We are a disgraced, crushed people. We cannot even raise our heads and say *Shema Yisrael* in public."

The street narrowed. At every doorway stood a cauldron of bright dye—crimson, indigo and green. Skeins of freshly dipped silk were hung up to dry and dripped into the gutter, and the brightly colored water ran downhill to the river.

"This is the dyers' quarter," ibn Hassan explained.

At a break in a wall, they saw a factory where the world-famous Moroccan leather was made. This was a large court-yard, filled with adjoining stone vats. The vats were filled with saffron for yellow, poppy for red, indigo for blue and antimony for blue. Sweating men in loincloths bent over, dipping hides. All about the tannery, rooftops were hung with drying hides.

The air was nauseating with the odor of the animal skins and the dye mixed with cow urine (which was added for preservation). Ibn Hassan now led them across narrow walk-ways and over a bridge, until they arrived at a high-walled house. "This shall be your home in Fez. It is only a few minutes' walk from the home of Rabbi Yehudah ibn Shushan."

They entered a zigzag passage to a small patio shaded by a vine, in the midst of which flowed a small fountain, and went into one of the two rooms that opened off the fountain.

The floors were covered with woolen carpets, on which were placed velvet-covered divans. On the walls hung silk sheets.

Ibn Hassan pointed out an ornate chest at the end of the room. "You may keep your clothing there."

Rabbi Maimon's wife and daughters walked through the house to look at the storeroom. Here olive oil, honey and dried fruits were kept in large corked jars.

In the afternoon, Rabbi Maimon and his two sons paid a visit to Rabbi Yehudah ibn Shushan. Walking down a narrow lane shaded by whitewashed walls, they came to a nondescript house where a young man at the door wearing a black fez and white robe looked at them suspiciously. But when he saw ibn Hassan, he opened the wooden door and let them in.

At the end of the twisting passage, they came to a large courtyard whose floor was a mosaic of violet squares on white, with a small eight-sided star at the corner of each square. On the opposite side of the courtyard sat a *chacham* in a red fez and white long blouse covered by a tan robe. About him sat a cluster of twenty boys and young men. He was chanting the words of the Talmud and then adding his explanation.

Rabbi Moshe joined the other students.

Here, at the risk of his life, Rabbi Yehudah ibn Shushan taught the sacred words of the Torah. Every student knew that his life too was at stake; for if anyone denounced them, they would be executed.

The following day, Rabbi Moshe was led by a fellow student to the Kairouyine medical study groups. Rabbi Moshe's companion led him confidently through a pavilion and into an austere room with tens of horseshoe arches over plain columns.

Here taught the leading physicians of Islam, men whose knowledge and ability was centuries ahead of the craft practiced in the Christian lands.

After an examination, Rabbi Moshe was allowed to join the medical study groups.

Every day, Rabbi Moshe led a double life. For part of the day, he would learn Torah in secret with his father and Rabbi Shushan. Then he would come to the Kairouyine Medical School and mingle with Muslims and other secret Jews in order to learn the medical sciences.

One day, Rabbi Moshe went to the Kairouyine Library. Here was one of the most magnificent collections of Islamic literature in the world: poetry, history, music, philosophy, theology, engineering, agriculture—and medicine.

"May I help you?"

Rabbi Moshe had been searching among the stacks of medical manuscripts. He looked up at the voice: it was an older man, dressed in a muted style. His beard was combed to a point, and his clothes gave off the scent of saffron.

"I am looking for Chunayn ibn Ischak's translation of Hippocrates' Aphorisms."

"A good text to study." The man leafed through the manuscripts with neat, small fingers and handed a book to Rabbi Moshe.

"Thank you."

"My name is Abu Alarab ibn Muisha. I hear you talked of well in the medical community."

Rabbi Moshe bowed his head. "You honor me. And who has not heard of your magnificent writings on Muslim thought or read with delight your sugared verse?"

Ibn Muisha smiled. "You mention my theology before you do my poetry."

"Certainly. For is the knowledge of G-d not greater than the pleasure of scented words?"

Late at night, Rabbi Maimon returned home. It was hard to find his way in the dark, across the bridge over the black river, past the now-silent tannery and marketplace. At last, Rabbi Moshe pushed open the heavy door and entered the dark courtyard. In his father's apartment, a light shone from the charcoal-burning metal brazier.

Rabbi Moshe walked into the room. His father was sitting with his face in the shadow, his chin sunken on his hand.

"Father, what is it?"

56

"I have been thinking of the dreadful state of the Jews here in Fez. G-d have mercy! We are losing an entire generation. I will do whatever I can—but what can I do?" He fell silent. "The help I tried to give here forty years ago did not do much good."

"What happened then, Father?"

"Sit, my son, and I shall tell you."

Rabbi Moshe sat before his father. The light of the coals flickered, casting shadows across his features.

"This took place about fifteen years before you were born, Moshe. A pious, wise and learned man came to Spain from Dera, Morocco, to learn under my teacher, Rabbi Yosef ibn Migash.

"After that, he came to Fez. Many people turned to him because of his piety and wisdom.

"One day, Rabbi Moshe Deri announced that he had learned in a dream that the Mashiach would soon come. Because he was a good and wise man, many people were drawn after his words.

"I tried to get people to leave Rabbi Moshe Deri and warned them that they were making a mistake. But very few people listened to me.

"Rabbi Moshe Deri began to make predictions, all of which came true.

"One day—I believe it was in *Marcheshvan*—he predicted that a great rain of blood would fall that week. This would be the sign of the coming of the Mashiach, as in the verse, 'I placed signs in the heavens and earth of blood and fire.' (*Yoel* 3:3)

"That very week, there was a torrential downpour of water mixed with dirty red mud, so that it appeared bloody.

"Now almost everyone believed that Rabbi Moshe Deri was a prophet—and we learn that prophecy will return before the coming of the Mashiach.

"Rabbi Moshe Deri then predicted that the Mashiach would arrive on the *Seder* night. He told everyone to sell their possessions and to take loans from the Muslims—as in the verse, 'They borrowed from the Egyptians vessels of silver, etc., and they despoiled Egypt'." (*Shemos* 12:35-36)

"And that is what the people did?" asked Rabbi Moshe.

"Yes! Almost all the Jews sold their possessions and took loans from the Muslims."

"What happened on the *Seder* night?"

Rabbi Maimon sighed. "Nothing happened, my son. People were lost and desperate. Their hearts were broken because the Mashiach hadn't come. They had only a few possessions left, and many debts.

"When the gentiles found out about this, they wanted to find Rabbi Moshe Deri and kill him.

"Rabbi Moshe Deri had to escape from Fez. But before he did, he predicted everything that would happen in North Africa, both great and small. Finally, he made his way to Eretz Yisrael, where he passed away—may his memory be for a blessing.

"And now, after such a calamity, to be suffering such persecution—it's too much! What consolation can this people have?"

(This episode is told by the Rambam at the end of his *Igeres Teiman*—see the version in *Igros Harambam*, edited by Isaac Shailat. Some date this story later, in the 1160s, at the time that Rabbi Maimon was in Fez with Rabbi Moshe—*The Rishonim*, the *Encyclopedia Judaica* and *Harambam* by N. T. Sifrai. But *Igeres Teiman* clearly places this episode in the 1120s.)

The following day, ibn Hassan took them on a tour of the Jews of Fez. They passed a group of laughing Berber boys with big teeth, curly black hair and dusky skin. In the marketplace, a woman in a violet robe gave them a suspicious look. Only her eyes were visible behind a light-blue veil, embroidered with indigo, scarlet and white flowers.

Ibn Hassan stopped before the entrance of one of the many small mosques in the city. From behind the wall, they could hear the enthusiastic voices of small boys chanting verses from the Koran.

"Listen!" said ibn Hassan. "Most of these children are Jewish. Their parents have to send them here to learn under fear of death. Now come with me. I wish you to see something else."

"Out of the way!" The driver of a mule carrying a huge bundle of animal hides cried out his warning, and the three men pressed against the wall.

After a fifteen-minute walk, they arrived at a house from which came the strains of music. A servant showed them into the courtyard, which was crowded with tens of men. Ibn Hassan greeted a few men warmly, kissing them on both cheeks. Musicians played metal castanets, a cylindrical drum, wooden flutes, a zurna (similar to the oboe) and an oud, a type of lute.

They entered a reception room, where men reclined before platters of pigeon pie and lemon chicken. Some sipped *halib luz*, a drink made of almonds and milk.

At the head of the table sat a young man and next to him a young woman in her early teens, stiff and painted as a doll.

"A wedding feast," ibn Hassan told Rabbi Maimon and Rabbi Moshe. "It lasts for fifteen days. Look, you see the groom? He is Jewish. But he could find no Jewish woman to marry, and so he has married into a Muslim family. It is considered a good match."

In the street, Rabbi Maimon asked, "Why do you show me all this? Is it to break the heart of an old man?"

"Heaven forbid!" ibn Hassan exclaimed. "But surely your prayers can awaken the mercy of Heaven. And perhaps there is something that you will find to do to strengthen our people."

"I can try," Rabbi Maimon murmured. "As to whether I can have an effect, that will be in the hands of the Compassionate One."

In the evening, Rabbi Maimon began to compose his famous *Igeres Hanechamah*—the *Epistle of Consolation*.

"Dear brothers, Jews in suffering," Rabbi Maimon wrote, "may G-d have mercy on us soon. We need to know that the sufferings that G-d inflicts on people are the ultimate good.

"G-d has chosen the Jews from among all the nations. He will never exchange us or reject us for any other people. G-d is not like a man, who lies or reconsiders. Far may it be from us to think that He has cast us away and will no longer have compassion on us.

"We see that G-d chose the Jews and made us His firstborn. He turned to us and revealed His goodness to us. He came close to us in a way that no one else has ever experienced and that no one else will ever experience. From this, we learn that G-d knows that we will always be faithful and keep His *mitzvos*.

"The evils that we suffer today are merely passing circumstances. We must believe in G-d and His promises. In His own Name, G-d swore that He would raise us up. Let us not be upset by the might of those who torment us and the length of time that we suffer. From troubles will spring salvation, and from groaning will come tranquillity.

"We in the exile are like those who drown in the sea. The water has come up to our nostrils, and all about us is the sea of exile. But the rope of Torah and *mitzvos* is tied from heaven to earth, and every hand that grasps it has hope and security. When one grasps this rope, one's heart is strengthened, and one may hope for salvation."

Many Jews were deeply troubled that they had to pretend

60

to be Muslims in public. Did G-d condone such a way of life? Could they still be considered Jews?

In his letter, Rabbi Maimon assured these Jews that even a person who is forced to say his prayers in their shortest form; if he only performs *mitzvos*, he remains a good Jew. (*Chemdah Genuzah*)

Rabbi Moshe's *Epistle of Consolation* was surreptitiously distributed among the Jews of Fez, and it had a great effect.

Many Jews had all but given up hope of leading a true Jewish life. They had begun to doubt that there was a purpose to their keeping *mitzvos* or that G-d still cared for them.

Now Rabbi Maimon's letter reassured them. It gave them the feeling that their efforts to observe the Torah were meaningful and would bring them reward. They were strengthened in their belief that G-d and the Torah leaders still loved them.

Again on *Shabbos*, women made *cholent*—for a *Shabbos* without *cholent*, went the saying of Moroccan Jews, was like a king without a throne.

After *Shabbos*, Jews again gave each other fragrant sprigs to smell at *Havdalah*, and they again celebrated the *melavah malkah* with coffee pastry and *zemiros*.

On *Sukkos*, the chair of Eliyahu again was placed in the *sukkah*, covered with colorful embroidery, holding sacred books. On *Simchas Torah*, the men again danced with the Torah as the women threw sweets at them.

On *Chanukah*, the women again made jelly doughnuts, and on *Purim*, Haman was again burned in effigy.

And on *Shavuos*, again a few *matzos*, saved from *Pesach*, were shred into bowls of milk and honey, for the Torah itself is like milk and honey.

5

The Letter

RABBI MOSHE CONTINUED TO LEARN UNDER RABBI IBN SHUSHAN and to work on his *Pirush Hamishnayos*. Among his colleagues was the famous Rabbi Yosef ibn Aknin, who authored a Commentary on *Shir Hashirim*.

It is possible that about this time, Rabbi Moshe married and had two children. But the circumstances are not clear.

He also continued his medical training (a trainee typically spent ten years studying medicine), and he became an accomplished physician. In his later *Treatise on Asthma*, Rabbi Moshe described discussions he held with well-known Moroccan physicians who were his colleagues, both Jewish and Muslim. He mentioned among others the Jewish physician Abu Yusuf ben Muallim and the Muslim Muhammad, son of the famous Avenzoar.

Among the Arabs, Rabbi Moshe was known as Abu Amran

Musa—a gifted physician and philosopher.

Rabbi Moshe sat in the study group one day, listening to the doctor, "In sum," the wizened man was saying, "Abulcasis teaches us that one should never undertake surgery until there is proof that the usual treatments are not effective. If the physician has not diagnosed the nature of the illness and has been unable to determine its cause, it is a crime to attempt an operation, which may endanger the life of his fellowman."

The students shifted impatiently. They had learned this the previous semester. Now they waited for the lecturer to begin to speak on the course topic of herbs and diet.

The lecturer began talking of foods. "Warmth, coupled with dryness, will make the physical condition bilious; but when coupled with wetness, it will produce thin-bloodedness.

"The fig has warmth and wetness of the first degree. The best variety is the white fig, with a split mouth. These are used for the kidneys, as they dissolve the sand in them.

"The plum has coldness to the first degree. It is used to evacuate the bile.

"The pear has coldness to the first degree, and dryness to the second degree. It is used for stomach weakness."

The sun was shining through the western windows and Rabbi Moshe began to think about *Minchah*.

". . . There are four humors in the body: the yellow bile, the blood, mucous and black bile, corresponding to the four natural properties of warm, cold, wet and dry. These are the four natural impulses to expansion and contraction, fluidity and solidification."

There were shouts, and a cluster of people burst into the chamber. The lecturer stepped back, and the students leaped to their feet.

Two Almohad soldiers had hold of a student. One of them held him from behind, his arm around his neck. The other soldier, breathing hard, had a welt on his cheekbone. "Our apologies for interrupting," he said to the doctor. "You will be glad to know that we have uncovered this secret Jew whose presence was defiling the holy mosque."

The doctor and the young men looked back in silence, and moments later, the two soldiers dragged the student out of the building.

"Ahh . . . where were we? These interruptions . . . Oh yes. The violet has coldness to the first degree . . . "

In the years that had passed since Rabbi Maimon had written his *Igeres Hanechamah*, his *Epistle of Consolation*, Almohad persecution had grown worse. There was nothing one could do to protest without forfeiting one's own life.

The more fortunate Jews, such as Rabbi Maimon and Rabbi Moshe, never having been known in Fez as Jews, were assumed to be Muslim and were generally ignored by the government. They were never interrogated or investigated, and therefore, they were free to live as Jews without professing any allegiance to Islam.

Again, Jews were confused and distraught. One of the hidden Jews of Fez sent a letter to a famous rabbi who lived outside of Fez, where the terrible decrees were not in force. In this letter, the hidden Jew expressed the deadly dilemma that the Jews of Fez were facing.

"What is preferable?" the Jew asked. "Should we deny the religion of Mohammed and die for the sanctification of G-d's name?

"Or should we declare our allegiance to Islam, while secretly keeping the *mitzvos*? Many Jews have chosen to do this. They go to the mosque, but they also pray secretly in synagogues. Is this the proper course of action?"

The rabbi replied, "A person must deny that Mohammed is a prophet, and must allow himself to be killed.

"Whoever declares that Mohammed was a prophet is like a denier of the G-d of Israel. Whether or not he keeps all the *mitzvos* of the Torah, he is considered a non-Jew. Even if he was forced to make that statement, he is wicked, and he is to be counted among those who are unfit to give testimony.

"You asked about a person going to the mosque and then praying in a secret synagogue. The prayer of such a person is worthless. More than that, it is a sin added to his previous transgression. This is similar to the verse, 'My people have committed two evils against Me: they have bowed to an image and bowed to a temple.' (*Yirmiyahu* 2:13) After entering a mosque, which is like bowing to an image, going into a synagogue—bowing to a temple—is also considered an evil."

Rabbi Moshe came home one evening. In his study, he studied Aliscander's commentary on Aristotle. Aristotle, Rabbi Moshe wrote later, gained the highest knowledge a man can attain without divine inspiration.

Then, from the other room, he heard the sound of muffled sobs.

He put down the book and went to the door. "Miriam, what's wrong?"

His sister raised her eyes, lowering her hands from her face. "It's ibn Hassan. He says that he is going to give up his life for the sake of G-d."

"What are you talking about?"

"He came here looking for Father, but Father was out. He said that according to *halachah*, he was obligated to go to the Muslim authorities and tell them that he is a Jew and does not believe that Mohammed is a prophet—and then they will kill him!" She gave a sob. "And on top of that, his heart is broken because of his children."

"What do you mean?"

"He says that when he told his children that they too will have to give up their lives, they said that they wouldn't go. They said that since whenever they do a *mitzvah*, it is considered a sin before G-d, they are casting the Torah away completely and becoming Muslims."

"This is terrible!" Rabbi Moshe said. "What about Father's *Epistle of Consolation*?"

Miriam shrugged her shoulders. "Ibn Hassan said that conditions are different now, that he has to follow the *halachah* of this latest letter."

This *"Epistle of Zealousness"* that had been sent to Morocco caused havoc. Those who sincerely served G-d felt that they and their families must die for the sake of sanctifying the Name of G-d. Others, whose service of G-d was more perfunctory, felt that they would be sinning less by giving up a hypocritical double-life and becoming true Muslims.

Rabbi Moshe was inflamed with passion. How could that rabbi, who did not know firsthand the conditions under the Almohads in Fez, give such a *Halachic* decision? How could he write such a letter that would destroy a thousand-year-old community?

His letter was, besides, an attack on the gentle, tolerant tone of Rabbi Maimon's *Epistle of Consolation*.

Rabbi Moshe set himself the task of responding to the *Epistle of Zealousness* and attempting to save the Jews of Morocco.

Why didn't Rabbi Maimon himself respond to the *Epistle of Zealousness*? Perhaps he felt that it would seem as though he were engaged in a personal vendetta. (It is also possible that this letter was written a few years later, when Rabbi Moshe was already in Egypt, after the death of Rabbi Maimon.)

In the dim light of the brass oil lamps, Rabbi Moshe sat down on the divan in his room and began to write:

"Someone has asked a question of a wise man—that is, a man who is wise in his own estimation, a man who never experienced what the majority of Jewish communities have experienced during this period of forced apostasy."

The next day, a middle-aged man stood in his house,

reading to his sons and sons-in-law. " . . . The rabbi answered weakly, with no reason to his words, not speaking to the point, making statements that even an ignoramus would not make . . . "

A scholar read the letter to a group of craftsmen in the back of a poorly lit shop.

" . . . Now I will explain how this person didn't realize what he is doing. He thought that he was doing a *mitzvah*, but he committed many sins.

"When the Jews were in Egypt in the time of Moshe Rabbeinu, they abandoned their faith and, with the exception of the tribe of Levi, gave up the *mitzvah* of circumcision and were at fault in marital laws. But when Moshe said, 'They will not believe me,' (*Shemos* 4:1), G-d punished him, saying, 'They are believers and children of believers,' but in the end you will lack faith in Me. (*Shabbos* 97a)

"In the time of Eliyahu, with the exception of seven thousand people, all the Jews worshipped idols. But when Eliyahu denounced them, G-d rebuked him, 'Before denouncing Jews, you should denounce the other nations.' Now, 'Go, return to the desert of Damascus.' (*Melachim I* 19:15)

"In the time of Yeshayahu, the Jews sinned even more. They worshipped idols, spilled blood and disgraced the Name of Heaven. But when Yeshayahu said, 'I dwell among a nation of unclean lips,' (*Yeshayahu* 6:5), he was punished, and he wasn't forgiven until Menashe killed him, as our Sages said. (*Yevamos* 49b)

"When an angel complained that Yehoshua ben Yehotzadak's sons were marrying daughters not fit for Kohanim, G-d distanced that angel."

A large group of *yeshivah* students gathered in Rabbi Shushan's *yeshivah* listened as one of them read Rabbi Moshe's letter.

"If such great leaders and the angels were punished for

speaking a few negative words, how can an unimportant person allow himself to speak against Jewish communities, teachers, students, Kohanim and Leviim, calling them sinners, evil-doers, non-Jews, unfit to give testimony and deniers of the G-d of Israel? What will be the punishment of a person who writes such words?

"These people did not rebel against G-d for pleasure. They did not abandon the religion for some momentary gain. They did what they did because of the outstretched sword, the taut bow and the pressure of war.

"This person does not realize that G-d will not abandon these people, who did not sin wilfully. G-d does not despise the poor man . . . "

In the courtyard of a private home, a family sat on the floor and cried as the son, the most learned among them, read the letter.

"Rabbi Meir was once captured during a time of religious persecution, and he was given ham to eat. He said, 'I will willingly eat it,' and pretended to eat. (*Avodah Zarah* 18b and *Koheles Rabbah*) In the eyes of this self-styled wise man, Rabbi Meir was a non-Jew!

"And there is a similar story about Rabbi Eliezer. So in the eyes of this self-styled kosher authority, Rabbi Eliezer was not fit to give testimony!

"In the present religious persecution, we are not required to worship idolatry, but only to say that we believe in the Muslim religion. The Muslims know that we do not believe in it, but that we are fooling the king, saying one thing and believing another.

"In the days of the evil Nevuchadnezzar, all the Jews in Bavel bowed to the idol with the exception of Chananiah, Mishael and Azariah. But no one ever called them evil-doers, non-Jews or unfit to give testimony. G-d did not consider them to have served idols, since they were forced.

"Under the evil Greeks, there were terrible decrees, including a law that no Jew may close his door so that he will not be able to do a *mitzvah* in private. Our Sages did not call the people non-Jews and evil-doers. Instead, they called them completely righteous and prayed in their merit, composing the prayer for *Chanukah*, 'You delivered the evil into the hands of the righteous' . . . "

Across Morocco, at thousands of gatherings, people listened to Rabbi Moshe's words.

" . . . Still, I would not have responded if that rabbi had not written that a secret Jew who prays does not have the reward of that prayer, and that to the contrary, he has committed a sin. I fear that this statement will, in the course of days, come into the hands of ignorant people who, reading that their prayer is not rewarded, will cease to pray. The same goes for other *mitzvos*, for from this man's words, one learns that such a person receives no reward for any *mitzvah* that he does.

"But let us look at Achav, who denied G-d and worshipped idols. When he fasted for two and a half hours (*Taanis* 25b), the Heavenly decree against him was nullified.

"When Eglon, king of Moav, the enemy of the Jews, gave honor to the Name of G-d, he was rewarded that Shlomo Hamelech came from his offspring, as will the Mashiach, and G-d did not withhold his reward.

"The evil Nevuchadnezzar, who killed the Jews like sand on the seashore and burned the Beis Hamikdash—because he ran four steps in order that G-d's Name would precede that of Chizkiyahu on a document (*Sanhedrin* 96a), he ruled for forty years, and G-d did not withhold his reward.

"Esav as well was rewarded for honoring his father.

"Now if these heretics were rewarded by G-d for the little good that they did, how much more the Jews, persecuted and forced to apostatize, who perform *mitzvos* in private!"

Rabbi Moshe now elucidated under what conditions a Jew

is obligated to sacrifice his life, what constitutes the desecration of G-d's Name and the sanctification of G-d's Name.

"Wherever our Sages said that a person should give up his life, if he was killed, he has automatically sanctified G-d's name.

"But if a person desecrated the Name of Heaven under duress, he is not liable to any of the seven punishments [given for transgressing negative commandments]. We have not found in the entire Torah that G-d punishes a person under duress. As our Sages said, 'A person under duress is not considered liable by G-d.'

"Such a person is not called a sinner, evil, or unfit to give testimony. All we can say is that he did not fulfill the *mitzvah* of sanctifying G-d's Name. He is called 'a person who desecrated G-d's Name under duress.' But he is in no way similar to a person who willingly desecrates the Name of Heaven . . . "

But practically speaking, what were the Jews to do? Behind a thousand walls, men continued reading from this letter.

"Therefore," Rabbi Moshe wrote, "whoever was killed rather than state that Mohammed is a messenger of G-d has great reward from G-d, since he sacrificed his life for the sanctification of G-d's Name.

"However, if someone asks if he should be killed rather than make that statement, we must tell him to make the statement and not be killed.

"But one must not remain in such a country. Instead, one must remain in one's house until one can leave that country. And if one needs to work, he should do so in private.

"One must keep whatever *mitzvos* one can. If it happens that a person sinned a great deal or desecrated the *Shabbos*, he now should still be as careful as he can. G-d repays one for all that one does: one is punished for every sin, and rewarded for every *mitzvah*.

"My advice to all those whom I love and who seek my counsel is that they leave this country. Go to a place where you can keep the religion and the Torah without any coercion or fear.

"Leave your house children, and all that you have. The religion that G-d has given us is great, and our obligation takes precedence over any factors that the wise regard as unimportant. Those factors do not last forever, but the command of G-d does last forever.

"One must leave behind everything that one has and travel day and night until one finds a place where one will be able to practice one's religion. The world is large and broad. As for someone who excuses himself because of his household and children—this is not a true excuse, for every individual is responsible for himself.

"One should move to the land of Israel and live there.

"There are those who fool themselves and say that they will remain where they are until the Mashiach will come to Morocco, and then they will leave with him for Jerusalem. But there is no set time for the coming of the Mashiach, and the obligation of our religion and *mitzvos* does not depend on the coming of the Mashiach.

"This is my opinion. And G-d knows the truth for sure."

Finally, Rabbi Maimon dealt with another issue. There were those people who, having scrupulously kept *Shabbos*, wanted to have nothing to do with those who had desecrated the *Shabbos*. Rabbi Moshe responded to this attitude by writing, "It is not correct to push away those who desecrate the *Shabbos* and to treat them with disrespect. Rather, one should draw them close and encourage them to keep the *mitzvos*. Our Sages said that if a person sinned wilfully, when he comes to the synagogue to pray, he is received and not treated disrespectfully. (*Tosefta Bava Kama* 7:3; *Mechilta Shemos* 22:3)"

This letter became known as *Igeres Hashmad*—the *Letter of Religious Persecution;* or *Igeres Kiddush Hashem*—the *Letter on Sanctifying G-d's Name.*

It became famous not only in Fez but all over Morocco. For generations to come, Jews turned to this letter for counsel on how to act during times of persecution.

Rabbi Moshe wrote in a style that revealed his great breadth of knowledge and was at the same time simple to understand.

The letter was filled with love for Jews, with compassion for those who had suffered and forgiveness for those who had been forced to transgress or who had allowed themselves to transgress the Torah.

6

Escape from Morocco

"Yes, ibn Hassan?"

They met on the whitewashed cobblestones. Drizzle fell incessantly from a gray sky.

Next to ibn Hassan stood a tall, husky man.

"This is Ovadiah ibn Youssuf."

Rabbi Moshe didn't say anything.

"Don't you recall?" ibn Hassan said. "Once I took you to his wedding."

"Yes, now I recall!" This was the young man who had married a Muslim girl.

"He has given up his wife. He is travelling with my family to Eretz Yisrael."

The young man looked at Rabbi Moshe with a brilliant smile.

"I am glad to hear of it," Rabbi Moshe said warmly.

"Rabbi Moshe," ibn Hassan continued, "ever since you have written your *Igeres Hashmad,* you have given a new heart to the people of Fez. Hundreds of Jews who had given up are now learning and keeping the Torah.

"And many hundreds of families have heeded your call to leave Morocco."

"If I may ask a question . . . " ibn Youssuf interjected.

Rabbi Moshe nodded.

"It would be my honor to travel with you to the holy land. May I?"

Rabbi Moshe shook his head. "I cannot say when I will leave. Since I am not known to the Muslims as a Jew, I do not have to make the oath. And in the meantime, I have much to do to help those Jews who are still here."

"But Rabbi Moshe," ibn Hassan said. "You cannot remain! If the Almohads hear of your *Igeres Hashmad* and discover that you are its author, they will kill you instantly, Heaven forbid!"

Rabbi Moshe merely nodded. "Good day, ibn Hassan. And good luck to you, young man."

Joy swept through the Jews of Morocco. It was almost as if the Mashiach were coming. Women folded sheets and clothing, men gathered together their goods and took stock of how much money they had, preparing for the trip to the Holy Land.

Jews began to stream out of Morocco, heading north for the dreary port city of Melilla, carrying beneath their voluminous robes the coins with which they would pay a merchant ship sailing for the Holy Land.

In the fort overlooking the city, the Almohad commander struck his fist into the air. "I want to know why the Jews are leaving Morocco. I want to know why they are abandoning Islam and returning to their infidel customs." He turned to a subaltern. "Remind me of the name of the chief rabbi."

"Yehudah ibn Shushan, sir."

"Go to his house and give him the choice of converting to Islam—or death."

"But sir—" The subaltern stopped and swallowed, amazed at his temerity.

"What is it?" the commander asked.

"It has been a tradition to treat the rabbi and his students with special respect, because he comes from the home city of Mahdi Tumart."

"Well, there is an end to every tradition."

"Yes, sir." The subaltern stepped to the door, when another officer entered, holding a number of sheets in his hand.

"Sir," the officer stepped before the commander. "I have discovered the cause of the Jewish desertion. Someone has been distributing this letter among them."

"Let me see it." The commander took the letter and leafed through it. "What does it say?"

"This letter incites the Jews to abandon Islam and leave Morocco."

"Find out who the author of this letter is and have him killed."

"Yes, sir."

"No, wait. Imprison him, and we shall put him on trial for heresy and treason. That will put fear into the hearts of the Jews."

"Yes, sir."

A few hours later, a company of soldiers broke into the courtyard of Rabbi Yehudah ibn Shushan.

"Jew!" the commanding officer barked. "Accept Islam or receive the sword!"

Rabbi Shushan looked into the officer's eyes. "I will live as a Jew."

"You mean that you will die as a Jew."

"Very well, then. I would rather die as a Jew than live as a Muslim."

The officer drew his sword and advanced upon the elderly *talmid chacham*. Before the horrified eyes of his students, Rabbi Shushan was stabbed to death and his bleeding, convulsing body fell to the ground.

"Perhaps this will put an end to your holiday!" The subaltern turned to his troops. "Round up these students. The commander wants to question them about the letter that has been circulating."

The soldiers marched out of the courtyard with the students, leaving behind the body of Rabbi Yehudah ibn Shushan, his red blood staining the mosaic tiles.

From inside one of the rooms arose a wail. A few minutes later, ibn Hassan crept out. Squatting before the body of the dead rabbi, he cried out, "These lips that taught Torah! These holy eyes! Who will comfort us?" He rocked back and forth hugging his calves, his head buried between his knees.

The sound of his wails brought others to the courtyard, and they too cried in grief.

"Come, let us carry the *chacham* onto his bed."

At these words, ibn Hassan came to. "I must warn Rabbi Moshe!" He slipped out of the courtyard and hurried to the house of the Maimons.

"Abu Amran Musa!" Ibn Hassan pounded at the door, as he called out Rabbi Moshe's Arabic name. There was no reply, and he pushed against the door, but the heavy bolt was in place. "Abu Amran Musa!"

A servant came to the door.

"Quick, let me in," said ibn Hassan. "It is a matter of life and death."

The servant blocked the door. "What is it?"

"The government has discovered the *Igeres Hashmad*. As

soon as they discover that Rabbi Moshe has written it—"

"Rabbi Moshe has already fled."

"Where is he?"

"I'm sorry. I cannot say."

According to the tradition of the Jews of Morocco, Rabbi Moshe hid with his family in an attic in the old section of what would become the Jewish quarter, Fez Elbali. Here Rabbi Moshe continued writing his *Pirush Hamishnayos*. A student used to bring them food at the risk of his life. *Ner Maarav*, written by Rabbi Toledano (of our time), reports that the Jews of Morocco had a tradition of exactly where Rabbi Moshe and his family had stayed, and that it was considered a holy place. Jews lived on that street until 5598/1957.

According to tradition, Rabbi Moshe remained in hiding for six months.

One day, soldiers surrounded the street where Rabbi Moshe and his family lived. Entering every house, they went from room to room. At last, the soldiers discovered Rabbi Moshe, who stood next to his trembling wife and two small children.

"Abu Amran Musa?" one of the soldiers asked.

"That is I."

"We have a warrant for your arrest as the author of a document inciting heresy and sedition."

A few days later, Rabbi Moshe stood before a military tribunal. The military commander, in a red fez and a white blouse covered by a crimson cloak, was delivering his summation.

"In light of the many serious charges brought against the defendant, Abu Amran Musa—to wit, that he is a secret Jew who has incited heresy and emigration of the population of Fez, who has insulted Mohammed and challenged the authority of the nation of Islam—the defendant, Abu Amran Musa, is herewith condemned to death by the sword."

There was a commotion in the back of the tribunal chamber. "Wait a moment!"

"Guards!" the military commander snapped. "Silence that man!"

From the back of the room, the man called out, "I am Abu Alarab ibn Muisha. I demand the right to speak."

An officer whispered into the military commander's ear, and the commander straightened up. "Forgive me, sir. I did not realize that such a great scholar and man of G-d was at our proceedings."

Ibn Muisha came to the front of the room. "May I be allowed to speak?"

"As you wish."

"You have sentenced this man, Abu Amran Musa, to death on the most absurd charges imaginable. I have been acquainted with him for almost five years, since he was one of the most outstanding young doctors in our group. He is a theologian, an outstanding physician, an expert in astronomy and mathematics, and a deeply-learned philosopher. Most of all, he is a man who leads his life according to the tenets of sobriety and the worship of the Almighty G-d.

"In short, your honors, this man, Abu Amran Musa, is an outstanding Muslim. I have found few, if any, men of his caliber, whether in the medical community, the mosque—or the army.

"The charge that Abu Amran Musa is actually a secret Jew who has written this missive encouraging other Jews to apostatize is grotesque in the extreme." He turned to the commander. "If you put this great man to death, you will have committed a great evil against Islam. Rather than gaining fame, you will acquire the opprobrium of generations to come. But when you give him his freedom, you will gain the admiration of all faithful Muslims, for you will have given life to an outstanding follower of our prophet Mohammed.

"I speak not only for myself," ibn Muisha said. "I speak for all the intellectuals of Fez. Just as an army cannot march without food, so can it not rule without the support of the thinkers. Sir, you will lose the support of the entire intellectual class if this outstanding Muslim is put to death.

"Drop these charges, and let Abu Amran Musa return to his life: the life of a philosopher."

After several seconds of silence, the military commander turned to his officer. "Pending further investigation, the sentence of death against the prisoner, Abu Amran Musa, is suspended. Take him back to his cell, and we shall reconsider his case."

A few days later, the charges against Rabbi Moshe were dismissed, and he was allowed to go home. Again, he was free without once having to declare that he was a Muslim or denying the Torah. But the danger of remaining was becoming great.

Rabbi Maimon assembled his family in the reception room where they had in better days hosted *talmidei chachamim.*

"We are in danger at every moment that we remain upon this soil," Rabbi Maimon said. "Only by the grace of G-d was Moshe's life spared. As Moshe counseled the Jews in his *Igeres Hashmad,* we too will travel to the Holy Land."

"You are not young, Father," Miriam said.

Rabbi Maimon shook his head. "Yet it is impossible to remain."

(According to some, Rabbi Maimon passed away while still in Morocco. This is, however, contradicted by the information in a letter by Rabbi Moshe to Rabbi Yaffes Hadayan, written later in Egypt.)

7

Passage to the Land of Israel

THE HULL OF THE OVERLOADED *DHOW* WAS A CONFUSION OF BODIES and packages. A few oil lanterns in the darkness illuminated a face, a tattered *djellabah,* a sailor with a dirty sheet wound about his head as a turban.

The desperate Jews were still climbing over the ship's low railing and being herded into the dark, unventilated "great cabin" below the poop.

Among the Jews climbed Rabbi Maimon, supported by his two sons. "Make way for the rabbi!" they shouted.

A space was cleared on the deck, and Rabbi Maimon was helped to sit down on one of the teak chests that held the sailors' belongings. Barefoot sailors rigged down the mast. With a soft, tearing sound, a large sail unrolled and billowed. The boat rocked suddenly, and the Jews at the bow grabbed whatever was next to them to keep from being pitched over.

It was the fourth of *Iyar,* 4925 (April 18, 1165), a *motzei Shabbos.*

A few hours earlier, Rabbi Maimon had made *Havdalah* for his family. The candle had burned with the hopeful light of a new week. Now they must smuggle themselves out of Morocco.

The anchor was hauled up, and the rope cast off. With long poles, four sailors pushed the ship away from the dock, as the other sailors pulled the sail about. The sail filled with the breeze, and the lean ship pulled out of the harbor.

The next morning, the ship was sailing into the rising sun. Under the bright sky, the Jews looked about. The ship was one hundred and thirty feet long, with a sleek hull of Malabar teak. Belowdecks were barrels of merchandise: dates, rose marmalade, cinnamon and sugar. Barely above their heads were unfurled two lateen sails, triangular sails set on long, sloping yards. The wind was steady and brisk, and the ship sailed smoothly, never out of sight of the North African coast to starboard.

Some of the Jews were seasick and tried to cure themselves by stuffing papyrus in their nostrils and ears, or sniffing cut lemons. In the evenings, the ship anchored and the sailors lit a small fire in a clay-lined barrel, in which they broiled the small fish they had caught during the day.

For six days, the ship continued smoothly. Then on *Shabbos,* the tenth of *Iyar,* a heavy rain broke over the glassy sea. Gusts of wind churned up the ocean until it was a roiling mass of foam-fringed waves. The *dhow* yawed in the massive waves, and the sail fluttered madly before the driving wind, as the sailors struggled to furl it. Water smashed over the bow and swept across the deck. The Jews crowded together, squeezing down below decks in the fetid darkness as the ship pitched wildly, and they prayed.

On deck, the nakhoda was yelling instructions to the

sailors above the roar of the storm. Two sailors pushed with all their might at the ship's rudder. The prow smashed downward into the water so that the bow creaked and trembled, and the mast swayed dangerously. The entire *Shabbos*, the small craft was pitched upon the smashing waves, beneath a slate sky from which rain poured incessantly. The wind hurled the waves together wildly so that one could not tell the difference between sea and sky.

Then the rain faded away. The wind died down, and the choppy seas were calmed. A swift breeze pushed the clouds away, and the sun blazed down from the west. Only the soaked deck of the ship and the wretched cry of a child bore any reminder of the storm that had almost capsized the ship.

The sailors laughed and exchanged shouts with each other. One sailor claimed that he had heard one of the Jews whistling, which had brought on the winds. But the other sailors paid him no mind. With the help of the Compassionate One, they had been saved from the great storm.

The frightened passengers thanked G-d for their delivery from death. Among them, on the open deck of the ship running before the wind, Rabbi Moshe made a vow: "The date of my departure for Eretz Yisrael and the date of my delivery from this storm shall be a fast day for myself, my family and my offspring to the final generation. On this day as well, they should give charity according to their ability.

"In addition, every year, on the anniversary of our redemption from the storm, I will sit in seclusion, seeing no one. I will pray and learn the entire day as a remembrance that just as I did not find in the sea on that day anything but the Holy Blessed One, so shall I not see anyone and not sit with anyone."

The *dhow* sailed for another twenty-eight days, passing Algeria and Tunisia. Then the ship swooped southward to hug the coastline of North Africa, past the Gulf of Sidra, the hump of Libya and Egypt. Occasionally, the ship would come to port, where traders brought merchandise on and off the ship, and they took on fresh supplies of food and water.

There was a *shochet* on board. Once he slaughtered a goat that belonged to one of the passengers, and the freshly broiled meat was shared with the *nakhoda* and sailors.

(According to some, Rabbi Moshe and his family disembarked at Alexandria, Egypt, and from here travelled northeast to Eretz Yisrael.)

On the third of *Sivan*, a *motzei Shabbos*, the ship docked at nightfall at Acco, the central port of the Eretz Yisrael.

"On this day," Rabbi Moshe wrote later, "I vowed that this date shall be a day of gladness, joy, feasting and gifts to the poor for myself and my family to all generations." (Manuscript version of *Pirush Hamishnayos* on *Rosh Hashanah*)

The Jewish refugees stood on the stone dock of Acco in the dark lit by a few torches. Behind them, the sea slapped against the stone sea wall.

They were standing on the soil of the Holy Land! But they were cold, bedraggled and weary.

They spent the night in a poor hostel. The next day, Rabbi Moshe and his father walked through the sunny streets. Here, for the first time, Rabbi Moshe saw Christians, with their fair hair, pale eyes and plain robes.

There was a small number of Jews in the synagogue. Rabbi Moshe listened to their speech. They seemed mostly simple men. At the head of the synagogue, the rabbi was unwrapping his *tefillin*. Rabbi Moshe introduced himself and motioned to his father, who was still praying.

"Of course I have heard of your great father!" the rabbi said. "You must be my guests."

Walking to the house of Rabbi Yaffes ben R. Eliyahu Hadayan, Rabbi Moshe saw Jewish merchants sitting before their shops and a craftsman beating on a copper vessel.

In Rabbi Yaffes's sparsley furnished home, the men reclined at a breakfast of *leben,* bread and dates. Later, they walked about the town. A boy led a donkey laden with brambles past them. Clothing hung limply behind a stone house with a small penthouse on its flat roof.

"The situation here is not good for the Jews," Rabbi Yaffes said. "There are no more than a thousand Jewish families in all of the land of Israel—most of them poor. What can we do? After a hundred years of war between the Muslims and Christians, it is a wonder that a shred of grass still remains in the Holy Land. Here we are under the rule of Amalric I, a young man in his late twenties who calls himself King of Jerusalem, and who rules Yerushalayim, the Galil and the coast from Ashkalon to here. Woe that the Holy Land should have such a ruler!"

A Christian soldier rode past them on a gaunt horse. He was ragged and dirty, his hair greasy.

"The Christians and Muslims constantly attack each other," Rabbi Yaffes said. "And both of them will attack travellers. One must be very careful when travelling anywhere."

Over the course of the next five months, Rabbi Moshe grew close to Rabbi Yaffes. In a letter that he wrote to him later, he described him as "the man of wisdom and understanding, the discerning judge." "I will never forget," Rabbi Moshe wrote, "how we walked in the deserts and forests together, seeking G-d."

In their great love for Eretz Yisrael and its holy places, Rabbi Maimon, Rabbi Moshe and Rabbi David persuaded Rabbi Yaffes to tour the Holy land together with them.

On a Tuesday, the fourth day of *Marcheshvan,* the four men set out from Acco, putting their lives in jeopardy.

Two days later, they arrived in Yerushalayim. There, the four men stood near the Har Habayis and prayed with awe and trembling. Rabbi Moshe later wrote in the *Mishneh Torah,*

"Even though the Beis Hamikdash today is destroyed, a man is required to treat it with awe, just as when it was built." (*Beis Habechirah* 7:5)

They remained in Yerushalayim for three days, getting to know the two hundred Jews who lived near Migdal David, in the ruin that the Crusades had wrought. These Jews had no way of earning a living and were forced to rely on charity from Jews outside Eretz Yisrael. Everywhere, Crusaders in shirts on whose sleeves were emblazoned red crosses passed through the streets, rowdy and coarse.

The four men continued their dangerous journey southward. "On Sunday, the ninth of *Marcheshvan*," Rabbi Moshe recorded, "I left Yerushalayim for Chevron, to kiss the burial places of my forefathers in the Cave of the Machpelah."

Unlike the situation afterward, Rabbi Moshe and his companions were able to enter the cave. "That day I stood in the cave and prayed, praise be to G-d for everything."

A contemporary of Rabbi Moshe, the famous traveller Binyamin of Tudela, wrote that the first two sections of the cave were empty. The third had six stones, on which were carved: "This is the tomb of Avraham"; "This is the tomb of Yitzchak ben Avraham Avinu"; "This is the Tomb of Yaakov ben Yitzchak ben Avraham Avinu"; "This is the tomb of Sarah"; "This is the tomb of Rivkah"; and "This is the tomb of Leah."

Just as he had rejoiced to enter the Holy Land itself, so did Rabbi Moshe rejoice to visit the holy sites. "On these two days, the sixth and ninth of *Marcheshvan*—when I came to Yerushalayim and when I came to Chevron," Rabbi Moshe wrote, "I vowed that I will arrange a celebration filled with prayer and joy in G-d, filled with eating and drinking. May G-d help me in everything and help me fulfill my vow.

"And as I merited to pray amidst the ruins, so may I and all Israel soon see consolation, amen."

The four men travelled back north on the wild, unguarded roads, passing rocky hills that had once been verdant forests where lion and bear had roamed. Now only Bedouins wandered on the hills, and their flocks of black sheep destroyed the vegetation.

Rabbi Maimon and his sons returned to Acco.

Before Rabbi Moshe had left Morocco, he had written in his *Igeres Hashmad* that the Jews should come to Eretz Yisrael. He himself had marked his voyage here with days of fasting and days of celebration.

But he was grieved to acknowledge that his love for the land must be tempered with bitterness. "We can no longer remain here," his father told him soon after they had returned to Acco. "For our many sins, the land is downfallen and poor. We could only become a burden to the other Jews already here, or else become dependent on the charity of Jews outside the land."

With a heavy heart, Rabbi Moshe nodded. Avraham Avinu had been shown Eretz Yisrael only to be forced to descend to Egypt because of a famine.

A few days later, they packed up their belongings and again went to the harbor. It was not possible to travel upon the roads southward through the Negev and the Sinai Desert, because of the marauders and bandits.

But travel by sea was scarcely less dangerous. Besides the threat of storms, there was always fear of being assaulted by the crew—not to mention the pirates who overran merchant and passenger ships, stealing their possessions and holding Jews hostage for ransom.

Summer was coming to an end, and a stiff wind blew from the sea.

The day came when Rabbi Moshe and his family had to leave.

"We're setting sail!" the *nakhoda* yelled and turned his

back to the family on the dock.

Rabbi Moshe threw his arms about Rabbi Yaffes. "May G-d grant you success in all that you do."

"G-d protect you," Rabbi Yaffes replied. "May your journey be swift and safe."

Rabbi Moshe stepped onto the ship. A moment later, the other members of his family boarded the ship. Slowly, the figure of Rabbi Yaffes disappeared from view, and Acco's sea wall faded into a blur of obscurity.

8

Alexandria

THE SEA WALL OF ALEXANDRIA GREW CLEARER AS THE SMALL, ONE-sail *dhow* tacked and hove to shore. Small boats belonging to fishermen and pearl divers rocked on the choppy water. As the *dhow* approached the harbor, the passengers saw a lively, confident city.

Alexandria, like Cordoba and Fez, was Muslim—but it was two thousand miles farther to the east, and near the heart of the empire.

On the dock, amidst the scramble of sailors, fishermen and merchants, Rabbi Moshe's family hired donkeys to carry their possessions.

"Where is the Jewish quarter?" they asked a passing Jewish trader.

"Come with me," the Jewish trader replied, and he led them along the docks.

Alongside one ship, a group of Jews and Muslims stood before sailors standing on a rough, wooden platform. Two sailors held the arms of a young man, his garment torn and dirty, his head bent to the ground.

"Pirates," the guide told Rabbi Moshe. "They captured that boy. Our community will have to ransom him or else he'll be sold as a slave. It happens every day, and we don't know where we'll get the money to redeem all these captives."

The next day, Rabbi Moshe visited the great synagogue of Alexandria, which contained chambers for various *minyanim* of different trades: land owners, fruit growers, clothiers, dealers in ship stores.

Here was a community stemming from the times of the second Beis Hamikdash, when the great Jewish philosopher Philo had made the city famous. At that time, a million Jews had lived in Egypt among a population of eighteen million Egyptians. Now, about thirty thousand Jews lived in all of Egypt, and about three thousand in Alexandria: well-off artisans, merchants and shipowners.

Here they had political and religious rights unmatched by Jews in any other land.

Rabbi Moshe's brother, Rabbi David, went to the harbor one morning to speak with the merchants.

The guide at his shoulder was a small, swarthy man with a thick beard that pushed out in all directions. As they stepped in and out of the sunbeams that shone through the carpenters' quarter, Rabbi David asked, "Who is the leader of the Egyptian community?"

They were passing stores where the scent of tea mixed with the fumes of strong Turkish coffee. Merchants sat cross-legged in their shops, puffing at softly bubbling water pipes.

"He is called the *nagid*."

"Does he have any power?"

Raising his chin proudly, the guide said, "He is the ruler of the Jews. He must approve all religious and public appointments. He is also the head judge. He has the right to punish a Jew with prison or even whipping. And he represents all the Jews of Egypt to the Egyptian government. I'd say that that's real power."

"What is the name of the current nagid?"

The guide lowered his head and rubbed his beard. "Well, right now we don't have a *nagid*."

"Why not?"

They turned a corner, and the salty smell of the sea blew up to them. From high above their heads came the keening of a white seagull.

"About seven years ago, an evil Jew named Yahya Zuta denounced Nagid Shmuel to the Caliph as a traitor. Nagid Shmuel was removed from his post and Zuta took over. Sixty-six days later, Nagid Shmuel got his position back. But there has been so much fighting over the role of *Nagid* that after Nagid Shmuel died seven years ago, in 1159, no one has been *nagid*."

A little Arab boy ran up to the men, holding out a sack. "Pistachio, misters? Almonds? Fresh, fresh!"

Meanwhile, Rabbi Moshe's mastery of medicine and philosophy became public knowledge. One day, an Arab intellectual came to his home. "On behalf of my colleagues, we would like you to address our medical study groups on a regular basis" (as reported by the Arabic historian, Alkopto, who wrote on Rambam's life thirty years after his death).

The medical community of Alexandria was an ancient institution that was famous all over the world.

"Here you may speak as a Jew!" the Arab intellectual assured Rabbi Moshe. "Here you will find cultured, civilized Muslims."

But the following week, when Rabbi Moshe walked through the streets of Alexandria, his heart was anxious at the spiritual state of the Jews.

"Rabbi Moshe!" a voice called out.

It was that same Arab intellectual. Again he praised his city, the center of culture, breeding and wisdom. Before them strolled three Jews in brocaded silk robes, one with his hands folded behind his back.

"You see, Rabbi Moshe, how well we Muslims here treat the Jews—you see how wealthy and successful a Jew may become."

"Yes, yes."

"What is the matter, Rabbi Moshe? Certainly you agree?"

Rabbi Moshe started from his thoughts. "Agree?" He gave a strained smile. "Of course—quite gracious, quite."

The three wealthy Jews were Karaites, followers of a sect that had been started in the eighth century. They were more wealthy and numerous than the Jews who followed *halachah*—the rabbinic Jews. While the rabbinic Jews had no strong leaders to guide them, the Karaites were organized and powerful, and growing numbers of Jews were leaving *halachah* to join their movement.

In Alexandria, Rabbi Maimon replied to questions sent to him from all over the world. He completed as well a commentary on the Torah, a work on the laws of ritual purity and a commentary on an Arabic book on astronomy.

Rabbi Moshe continued his work on his monumental *Pirush Hamishnayos*.

And Rabbi David engaged in business as well as in the craft of being a *sofer.*

A half year later, Rabbi Maimon died.

The greatest scholars attended the funeral. All stores were closed. Rabbi Maimon was borne to the cemetery southwest of Mount Almukattem, one of the oldest Jewish cemeteries in the world, as professional mourners wailed and Rabbi Maimon's family walked alongside the body. At the cemetery,

Rabbi Maimon's body was laid directly into the ground without a coffin.

On the following *Shabbos*, the Jews gathered about Rabbi Maimon's family and offered them condolences.

From all over the world came letters of condolence—from the Christian countries and from North Africa.

Rabbi Maimon had been one of the greatest *talmidei chachamim* of his generation. He had been not only Rabbi Moshe's beloved father but his principal teacher as well.

Rabbi Moshe returned to the *beis midrash* of Alexandria. But even here, in the cool chamber where the colonnades rose to the ceiling like silent, timeless witnesses, the chaos of history intruded.

In 1166, Amalric, King of Jerusalem, marched against Cairo. But he was opposed and defeated by another enemy of Egypt, Shirkuh, general of Damascus, at whose side rode a general named Saladin.

Then in early 1167, Shirkuh, again with Saladin at his side, set out to conquer Cairo. But after fighting through a terrifying sandstorm, the army found that Egypt was being protected by the Christian Amalric, who had been paid the enormous fee of four hundred thousand gold dinars.

For hundreds of years, Islam had been divided into two principal warring factions: the orthodox Sunni Muslims, who ruled Syria, and the Shiite Muslims, who controlled Egypt. (Both the Almoravides and the Almohads, who had fought in Spain and Morocco, were part of the Sunni group.)

The Christians, Sunnis and Shiites battled each other, forming temporary alliances, betraying one to the other and engaging in assassinations and trickery.

Rabbi Moshe had fled two thousand miles from Spain and Morocco. But here as well, he was to find no peace.

The news of the entrance of Amalric into Cairo spread like wildfire through Alexandria. Everywhere people trembled:

with soldiers would come looting, wildness, death.

William of Tyre (historian and contemporary of Amalric) described the scene when the Christian delegation in Cairo appeared before Caliph Aladid, who was at the time sixteen years old:

"Escorted by the vizier and his armed retinue through the subterranean passages, the Christians passed through a succession of doorways guarded by Ethiopian slaves, to find themselves in a courtyard paved with stone mosaic. Its marble columns supported loggias [arcades] with fretted and gilded ceilings. Marble fish pools were filled with limpid waters, and they glimpsed exotic birds and strange beasts 'such as the mind sees in dreams.' As they approached the inner precincts of the palace they were awed and astonished by an increasing state of opulence. Pausing at last before the royal divan, the vizier prostrated himself three times and removed his sword; then, as curtains embroidered with pearl and gold were drawn aside, the caliph was dramatically revealed, seated in regal state on a golden throne."

The Christians now attacked the Syrian Muslims, but they were defeated south of Cairo.

The triumphant Syrians, led by Shirkuh and Saladin, headed north.

"Rabbi Moshe!" A Jew accosted Rabbi Moshe in the street. "Did you hear? The Syrians are headed for Alexandria. Do you think that there will be bloodshed?"

The Jew's companion interrupted. "There will be no fighting here. There is no great love among the Muslims in Alexandria for the Fatimids in Cairo."

Two days later, the hordes of Syrian forces appeared to the watchers on Alexandria's city walls: archers on horseback, camels carrying supplies, lancers, swordsmen, foot soldiers armed with swords and clubs.

There was no defense of Alexandria. When the Syrian

troops approached, the gates swung open before them. Soldiers raced through the deserted streets, pillaging stores and taking strategic positions.

A few days later, Amalric's Christian forces struggled out of the desert. But the gates of Alexandria were closed to them, and archers stood upon the city walls.

Amalric laid siege to the city. No food or water was allowed into Alexandria.

The inhabitants grew desperate and gaunt. Mothers had no milk for their children. Sick people died, and young people licked their lips, their tongues huge in their dry mouths.

In the midst of the siege, Shirkuh, commander of the Syrian forces, slipped out of Alexandria with most of his army in order to pillage other cities in upper Egypt.

Saladin was left behind with a force of a thousand men. In later years, he said, "What I went through in Alexandria, I shall never forget."

The famine grew worse. Saladin not only had to guard the city walls against the Christians, but against the inhabitants of Alexandria. Mobs of Alexandrians roiled through the streets. "Open the gates! Surrender to the Christians! But let us have food!"

Rabbi Moshe and his family were among the thousands of people who lacked food and water.

Saladin sent desperate messages to Shirkuh. At last, Shirkuh negotiated an accommodation with Amalric, and the siege was lifted.

A year later, the Jews of Egypt suffered tragedy again—this time one hundred and forty miles to the south of Alexandria, in Fostat, a great city two miles south of Cairo.

This was the city to which Rabbi Moshe would move in a matter of years.

In 1168, Amalric again entered Egypt. He attacked the city of Bilbeis, fifty miles northeast of Cairo. His troops rioted throughout the city, pillaging and stealing, and massacring the inhabitants of the city mercilessly. They even killed Christian Copts.

Desperate messengers fled the city and brought the horrific news to Cairo.

Shawar, vizier of Egypt, stood before his generals. "Amalric cannot take Cairo, for we are walled and well-defended.

"But we must not allow him to conquer Fostat."

This was what the generals had been waiting to hear. Fostat was a large city, a center of business, home to thousands of government officials. Amalric could gain incredible plunder here. Encamped within Fostat, he would have food, water and all the resources he needed to begin an extended campaign against Cairo.

Shawar walked out to the window and gazed south. Past the flat palace roofs, soldiers patrolled the city wall. He turned back to his generals. "We do not have enough troops to defend Fostat. So Fostat must burn. We must leave nothing for Amalric to make use of."

Fostat was also the home of thousands of Jews—both rabbinic and Karaite—who worked as merchants, craftsmen, physicians and in the palace of the Caliph.

In the next few days, soldiers poured into Fostat, carrying thousands of barrels filled with naphtha—clay grenades filled with mineral oil. They chased families out of their homes, buildings as high as fourteen stories.

An Arab eyewitness, Makrizi, wrote, "The people left in great haste, abandoning their possessions and their goods, in order to save themselves and their children. There was an impetuous flow of human beings; it seemed as though they were leaving their tombs for the Last Judgment. Fathers neglected their children and brothers were not each other's keepers. They went so far as to pay twenty dinars for a mount to take them from Fostat to Cairo. They camped in the mosques of Cairo, in the bathhouses, in the streets and on the roads. There they were, thrown together pell-mell with their wives and children, having lost their possessions and waiting for the enemy to bear down on Cairo. Shawar had twenty thousand pots of naphtha and ten thousand firebrands brought into Fostat. All of these were spread out in the city, and the flames and the smoke of the fire rose to the heavens. It was a frightening spectacle."

A soldier lit the wick of a naphtha barrel. He tossed it into a building. It crashed onto the floor and the blazing oil ran across the floor and licked at the wall-hangings, until they went up in a sheet of flame.

Soon, the entire room was an inferno of red and orange curtains of fire.

By the end of the day, all of Fostat was ablaze, a pillar of black cloud by day and a blazing pillar of fire by night.

For almost two months the fire raged, as in the streets of Cairo, over a hundred thousand refugees lived on the fetid streets, homeless amidst garbage and squalor.

Makrizi wrote, "The fire continued in the houses of Fostat for fifty-four entire days, as did the organized pillage carried out by slaves and sailors. For a long time after that, Fostat was a ruin called 'the hills of debris.'"

Meanwhile, Caliph Aladid appealed for help to the Syrian Muslims. Although they were his enemy, Amalric was their mutual enemy.

The Syrians responded. Shirkuh, accompanied by Saladin, joined forces with the Egyptians, and Amalric retreated to Eretz Yisrael.

Rabbi Moshe continued his Torah writing. It was Torah that lifted a man from the circumstance of events. One raised all the incidents of human life to G-d.

In 1168, Rabbi Moshe completed his *Pirush Hamishnayos*, which he called *Kiteb El Siraj*—in Hebrew, *Sefer Hamaor:*

The Luminary. It had taken him about ten years to write it. Rabbi Moshe was now thirty-three years old.

The work was written not for the scholar, but the average individual. Rabbi Moshe wrote in the language that would make the commentary most easily understandable in his surroundings: Arabic.

In his Introduction, Rabbi Moshe noted that he had written it "because I saw that the *mishneh* cannot be understood without basic knowledge of the Talmud, for the Talmud gives us general principles regarding the *mishneh* topic; or tells us that a *mishneh* is lacking some words; or that a *mishneh* is according to the view of a particular sage.

"A person cannot know the entire Talmud by heart, particularly when a *halachah* in one *mishneh* is discussed across a span of four or five pages. Then only an expert in learning can understand.

"Second, this work records the *halachic* conclusion of the *mishneh* and according to which sage that conclusion is reached.

"Third, the commentary provides overviews and discussions that lead a person to understand how to learn. The information and principles will be very useful in all areas of the Talmud.

"Fourth, it will serve as a useful review for a person who has already learned the material."

Rabbi Moshe wrote overviews to each tractate, and in his commentary, he utilized information from the entire body of Torah knowledge, as well as from scientific sources. He discussed such diverse topics as astrology, geometry, medicine and the calendar.

He had begun the work during his wanderings in Spain, and that experience had left its evidence in his commentary. Discussing whether after *Pesach* a Jew may eat leaven that a gentile had baked on *Pesach*, Rabbi Moshe noted, "The custom among us in Spain is to eat it." (*Pesachim* 2:2)

He had continued working on the commentary when he had moved to Morocco. In *Mikvaos,* he quotes the "scholars of Morocco," and in *Nedarim* and *Shavuos,* he quoted *halachah* taught "by the scholar here with us in the cities of Morocco."

He had continued to write the commentary during his short stay in the Holy Land.

And he had at last finished, in the land of Egypt.

He wrote at the end of the Commentary, "I worked on this while in the midst of unhappy circumstances, as part of the exile decreed upon us by G-d and wandering through countries, one end of the heavens to the other end. G-d knows that there are some *halachos* that I explained while travelling, and some I wrote while I was on the sea."

The *mishneh* itself exemplifies the lifting of human circumstance to Divinity. In its six Orders and approximately sixty tractates, our Sages discussed the entirety of Torah law as it applies to all of life. All aspects of living are connected to Torah and enhanced by being connected to Divine commandments.

In a number of long overviews, Rabbi Moshe presented an exposition of the Torah's outlook on vital areas of religious and spiritual meaning. By linking such overviews to his Commentary, he demonstrated that the *mishneh* is not merely a technical manual, but that it contains the rules that govern a life of meaning.

This was an age when Muslim intellectuals explained the dictates of the Koran within the context of the total meaning of a Muslim's life.

Rabbi Moshe had to show the Jewish student that Torah provides a world of meanings; that the *mishnayos* are contained within a framework of Divine intent that encompasses one's life.

Rabbi Moshe opened his Commentary with an essay of eleven short chapters on the transmission of the Torah.

Rabbi Moshe pointed out that "prophecy is of no advantage in explicating the meaning of the Torah and in deducing *halachah* according to the thirteen principles. The same process utilized by Yehoshua and Pinchas in learning and reasoning was employed by Ravina and Rav Ashi."

In Chapter Seven, Rabbi Moshe discussed the role of *Aggadah* in the Talmud and the need to serve G-d in wisdom.

"One should not think that the homilies in the Talmud are of little importance and lacking use. They have great understanding, since they contain great secrets that are lovely and wondrous, divine and true matters that the men of wisdom hid and did not desire to reveal.

"Regarding this wisdom, its explanation and how to deal with it, one must give oneself over to G-d and pray that He teach one and reveal the hidden secrets in the writing, as we find that David Hamelech prayed, 'Unveil my eyes and I shall gaze on the wonders in Your Torah.'" (*Tehillim* 119:18)

But what is the purpose of studying this Torah that G-d gave to Moshe Rabbeinu?

In Chapter Eight, Rabbi Moshe taught that the purpose of this universe is contained within man. The purpose of man is to attain wisdom and to serve and join other people who have attained wisdom.

Man, Rabbi Moshe wrote, "must realize the inner abstract meanings and to know the truth as it really is. With this wisdom, a person sees the inner meanings of things. Without such wisdom, a person is like an animal."

The most important such inner wisdom "is to have an awareness that G-d is One. All other wisdoms are only to sharpen the mind until one arrives at the knowledge of this divine wisdom."

In Chapter Nine, Rabbi Moshe returned to the Talmud. He

described the line of tradition since the closing of the Talmud: the Geonim, the Rif, Rabbi Yosef ibn Migash, his father and his own partially completed commentary on the Talmud.

"When the time came to me," Rabbi Moshe wrote, "I did all I could to gather the material written by earlier authorities, in order that I too would be able to work and receive reward from G-d. I gathered together all the explications of my father as well as all the material in the name of Rabbeinu Yosef Halevi.

"(The heart of that man in the Talmud strikes one with awe when one looks at his words and the depth of his intellect in deep studying.)

"I gathered my father's private notes. I also applied that which appeared to me correct from my own commentaries, according to my weak ability, and according to my knowledge of the sciences."

Rabbi Moshe also composed a famous Introduction to the chapter in *Sanhedrin* known as Cheilek—"portion"—after the statement, "All Jews have a portion in the World to Come."

In five chapters, Rabbi Moshe provided an overview of how the Torah views the great issues of meaning in life: reward and punishment, this world and the World to Come, Gan Eden, resurrection of the dead, the days of the Mashiach, and so on.

The purpose of learning Torah, Rabbi Moshe wrote, is "to love G-d your Lord." (*Devarim* 19:9)—"Whatever you do, do only out of love. This is the intent of the Torah and the basic intent of the Sages.

"Our Sages knew that this is very difficult and that not everyone can reach this level, since a person only acts in hopes of receiving some benefit or having some flaw removed. After all, how can a person be told, 'Do these things' and 'Do not do those things' not out of fear of G-d's punishment and not out of hope for reward? So the masses were allowed, in order to preserve their faith, to perform the *mitzvos* in the hope of receiving reward and to stay away from sins out of fear of punishment. As our Sages said, 'A person should always be involved in Torah even not for the proper intent, for out of this, he will come to the proper intent.'"

Rabbi Moshe went on to say that people are divided into three groups in regard to their having faith in the Sages. Only the third group, a very small number of people, have great faith. These people are very few. Calling them a 'group' would be like calling the sun one of the stars, when it is in its own class. These people are clear about the greatness of the Sages. They realize that our Sages do not speak empty words. They realize that their words contain both obvious and hidden meanings, and that whenever our Sages spoke about impossible matters, they spoke symbolically and allegorically.

Rabbi Moshe spoke of the difference between physical and spiritual pleasures. "Just as a blind person cannot understand color, a deaf person cannot imagine sound and a eunuch cannot imagine marriage, the body cannot understand spiritual pleasure.

"It is not fitting for those of us who learn Torah or for gentile mystics and philosophers to say that the angels, the stars and the heavenly spheres have no pleasure. In truth, they do experience a very great pleasure insofar as they know and are aware of the truth of the Creator. They experience an unending pleasure. They have no physical pleasure and they do not understand such a thing, since they have no senses as we do."

Rabbi Moshe now explained the statement of the Sages, "the reward of a *mitzvah* is a *mitzvah* and the punishment for a sin is a sin." One attains perfection by doing *mitzvos*. If one sins, one is held back from attaining one's completion. So "if you have performed a number of *mitzvos* in love and with effort, I will help you, says G-d, to perform all of them, and I will remove any stumbling blocks. But if you treat any of them contemptuously, I will bring stumbling blocks that will prevent you from performing all of them, until you will not reach your perfection and existence in the World to Come."

Rabbi Moshe presented short descriptions of a number of concepts that relate to the World to Come.

Gan Eden, Rabbi Moshe wrote, is "a fecund, fertile region on the globe. It has many rivers and fruit-bearing trees. G-d will reveal it to human beings in the future. He will show them how to arrive there, and people will take pleasure there. It is possible that people will find extraordinary plants that are extremely useful, wonderfully pleasant and sweet, in addition to those already known to us.

"This is neither impossible nor improbable but quite reasonable, even if it were not written in the Torah—and how much more so, since it is."

As for the days of the Mashiach, wrote Rabbi Moshe, "that is a time when the Jews will again have a government and they will return to Eretz Yisrael. They will have a great king whose name will be spread among the gentiles even more than Shlomo Hamelech.

"All the nations will make peace with him and all the lands will serve him, because of his great righteousness and the wonders that he performs.

"Whoever rises against him will be destroyed by Hashem and sent into his hand.

"There will be no change in nature whatsoever. The only difference will be that rulership will return to the Jews. As our Sages said, 'There is no difference between this world and the days of the Mashiach except for subjugation to the gentile nations.'

"In his days, there will be rich and poor, mighty and relatively weak. But it will be very easy for people to earn a living so that with just a little effort, a person will gain a great deal. As our Sages said, 'In the future, Eretz Yisrael will give forth cakes and fine garments.'

"The great advantage of those days shall be that we will have rest from the subjugation of the gentile rulers, which keeps us from performing all the *mitzvos*. Wisdom will increase, and wars will cease. There will be great spiritual perfection and we will attain the life of the World to Come.

"The Mashiach will die, and his son will rule after him, and then his grandson.

"His kingdom will last a very long time. Similarly, people will live for very long, since they will be free of worries and unhappiness.

"Do not be astonished that his kingdom will last for thousands of years. As our Sages said, 'The good gathering will not be quickly scattered.'

"But we do not desire the days of the Mashiach because of the great amount of harvest and wealth, nor in order to ride upon horses, nor in order to drink wine while listening to music, as the confused people think. The prophets and the pious ones desired the days of the Mashiach because of the ingathering of the righteous, the rule of goodness and wisdom, the king's righteousness and straightness, his great wisdom and closeness to G-d and the performance of all the *mitzvos* of the Torah, without laziness and without pressure."

And what is the ultimate purpose? "That is the World to Come," stated Rabbi Moshe. "But although it is the desired end, it is not fit for someone who wants to serve G-d out of love to serve in order to attain the World to Come. Rather, one should serve G-d in the following fashion:

"When one believes that there exists wisdom, which is the Torah, given to the prophets by the Creator; that there are good traits, which are *mitzvos*, and bad traits, which are sins— then, when a person has a straight nature, he will do what is good and avoid what is bad.

"When a person does this, he will perfect his humanity."

In the final chapter, Rabbi Moshe presented his famous Thirteen Principles of Faith.

"The first principle is to believe in the existence of the Creator.

"The second principle is G-d's oneness.

"The third principle is that He is not physical.

"The fourth principle is that G-d is the Primal Being.

"The fifth principle is that it is fit to serve G-d, to exalt Him, to make His greatness known and to perform His *mitzvos*.

"The sixth principle is that there are prophets.

"The seventh principle is that the prophecy of Moshe Rabbeinu is the greatest of all the prophets.

"The eighth principle is that the Torah is from Heaven.

"The ninth principle is that the Torah of Moshe was transmitted from the Creator.

"The tenth principle is that G-d knows the acts of human beings.

"The eleventh principle is that G-d gives reward to those who perform the *mitzvos* and punishes those who transgress the Torah.

"The twelfth principle is belief that the days of the Mashiach will come.

"The thirteenth principle is the resurrection of the dead."

Rabbi Moshe's *Pirush Hamishnayos* was a work that appealed to the layman and dazzled the scholar.

All across Egypt, the Commentary was studied. Copies were made and sent to Eretz Yisrael, Morocco, Spain, Yemen and Iraq.

Two students sat on the mats of an Alexandrian *beis midrash*.

"Have you seen Rabbi Moshe ben Maimon's Introduction to *Taharos*?"

"No, I haven't. But forget it. I tried learning *Taharos*. It is so complicated, I got completely lost. It will be many years before I want to tackle that again."

"That's where you're wrong!" the other student interrupted him. "Rabbi Moshe ben Maimon makes it all so simple—I mean, as simple as it could possibly be. He tells you the general principles and then shows how all the laws flow from them. Then he clearly shows you how the exceptions to the rule fit in."

"Really? I'll have to look at it. It was those exceptions to the rule that really threw me when I tried learning it the first time."

Two scholars walked along the waterfront of Alexandria's Eastern Harbor. Across the shining water, on a small island, stood the decaying stone debris of the Pharos. Fourteen hundred years earlier, it had been a great lighthouse, over four hundred feet high, with a polished mirror that cast a beam for thirty-five miles. Now it was a ruined tower whose blocks of weathered stone rose listlessly.

One of the scholars, Rabbi Eliezer, gazed across the water. "Look. That was one of the Seven Wonders of the World. Today this is one of the wonders of the world." He raised the manuscript in his hand.

"What is that?"

"It's Rabbi Moshe's Introduction to *Pirkei Avos, Shemoneh Perakim*. This should be learned in the synagogue every *Shabbos*!"

The other scholar, Rabbi Nachum, leaned his forearms on the railing, his fingers intertwined. Gazing at the boats in the swell, he said, "Yes, I have learned it." He turned to Rabbi Eliezer. "This small work does have the mark of greatness. It combines knowledge of Torah with great personal wisdom. And it speaks particularly to the people of our time."

"You mean the Aristotelians."

"Yes," said Rabbi Nachum. "The Muslims have brilliantly

adapted Aristotle's teachings to fit Islamic thought. But among us Jews, those of us who are thoughtful and analytical have had nowhere to go to in order to learn how Torah contains wisdom."

"Yes, I know," said Rabbi Eliezer. "The wisdom in the Torah is not set out and organized the way Greek wisdom is, *lehavdil*. So people have turned to Aristotle and to Muslim writings."

"In this little work," Rabbi Nachum said, "Rabbi Moshe does a wonderful job of talking about the meaningful things in life—about ethics and how to lead a good life, about how to keep one's soul healthy, about good and bad character traits, about serving G-d according to the golden mean. He shows rationally how one is to choose the good and discard the evil. He takes the complexity of life, of desires, of urges and ideals, and he presents a structure in which to understand them and in which to connect them to Torah and to G-d.

"He does all this in the context of the methodology of Aristotle. Now our bright young people will be able to see in Torah much more than that which they have seen in Aristotle, and they will not be tempted to abandon the study of the Torah—or, still worse, turn to the ways of the Karaites."

"I'll tell you what struck me," said Rabbi Nachum. "May I have a look at the manuscript a moment?"

Rabbi Eliezer handed Rabbi Nachum the manuscript, and he leafed through it.

"It was a quotation in Chapter Five. Ah, here it is!

"'A person must subjugate his spiritual powers in accordance with intelligence. He must always have one purpose in mind, which is to come close to knowledge of Hashem, to the degree that one is able to do so. All his acts should be so that his movements, his rest and everything bring him to this purpose, until he does nothing that is inconsequential.'"

Rabbi Nachum turned the page. "'He should intend when

he eats, drinks, when he goes to sleep and when he awakens, when he moves and when he rests that this be for the sake of keeping his body healthy.

"'The purpose of keeping his body healthy is that his soul will have a healthy, complete vessel with which to acquire wisdom and good character traits.'"

"Very wise," said Rabbi Eliezer.

"Wait. There's a little more.

"'A person shouldn't have in mind only self-satisfaction to the point that he picks the most tasty food and drink, as well as in other matters—but he should choose that which is most useful. If it is also tasty, so be it; or if it is not tasty, so be it.

"'Or he should choose that which is tasty according to the rules of medicine [for then that which tastes good is also useful]: like a person who has lost the desire to eat, he should awaken that desire with gourmet foods.

"'Similarly, someone who is overcome by depression should listen to songs and musical instruments and take strolls in the park amidst beautiful buildings, in the company of beautiful images and other such things that expand one's soul and remove the depression. His intent in all these things should be to heal his body.

"And the intent of healing his body is to acquire wisdom.

"Similarly, should one be engaged in acquiring money, one's purpose should be to spend it wisely [to give charity and to acquire wisdom], and to take care of one's physical needs so that one can live until one can understand Hashem as much as possible.'"

A breeze blew across the harbor, ruffling the water.

"What is it that you like so much about this passage?" Rabbi Eliezer said.

Rabbi Nachum closed the book and the two men resumed their walk along the harbor. "One sees here Rabbi Moshe's great personal wisdom and compassion. He understands that different men have different needs.

"In his Introduction to Cheilek, he spoke of music and poetry books as lacking in wisdom and being a waste of time.

"But here we see that Rabbi Moshe is both a teacher of Torah and a physician of the soul. He realizes that a person must live a life of Torah in a manner that fulfills his personal needs. So a depressed person must listen to music and spend his time taking walks in the park.

"Rabbi Moshe is a great Torah leader not only because he knows the Torah so clearly, but because he loves every Jew on his own level. Rabbi Moshe could have written a complex piece of Torah literature that would have dazzled other *talmidei chachamim*. But he has chosen to write not that which is impressive but that which is necessary."

"And you know something, Rabbi Nachum?" Rabbi Eliezer placed his fingers on Rabbi Nachum's arm. "It is the wisdom in this work that will survive when a thousand other writings, meant to be impressive, will have crumbled."

9

Saladin

IN CAIRO, CALIPH ALADID STILL RULED EGYPT. BUT WITHIN EGYPT stood the Syrian army under Shirkuh and his general, Saladin.

The year was 1169.

In the mosque, Shirkuh wrapped about himself the royal robe of honor that Caliph Aladid had presented to him in thanks for driving out Amalric.

He prostrated himself in the direction of Mecca.

In the muted, pious atmosphere of the mosque, Shirkuh thought back to Saladin at the army camp, south of Cairo. What was happening now? He burned to know if the plot had succeeded. Swiftly, he strode out of the mosque and swung onto his horse.

Meanwhile, Shawar, vizier of Caliph Aladid, was entering the army camp. At his side rode a guard, and behind them, soldiers bearing banners, drums and trumpets.

Shirkuh's troops, many of them Nubians and Sudanese, looked up at the passing Shawar with faded interest. He visited the camp every day.

To the west was the ruined silhouette of Fostat. Beyond that, on the other side of the Nile, rose the ancient Pyramids of Gizeh.

It was January 18.

A messenger stood at the entrance to Saladin's headquarters. "Sir, Shawar is approaching!"

"Is he? Good!"

Saladin strapped a short sword to his side. So, he thought to himself, when the cobra visits the fox often enough, he will learn that the fox has teeth.

How long was it since he had learned of Shawar's plan to assassinate Shirkuh?

The man was a fool! What was he waiting for, visiting every day with his clownish escort? He would learn the penalty of striking too late.

Saladin strode out to Shawar, who was riding up before the headquarters. Shawar's drummer played a staccato, and the trumpeter blew a fanfare.

Saladin tilted his head slightly in greeting.

Shawar looked at Saladin suspiciously. Is that a sardonic grin? Why does he wear that short dagger today?

Saladin gave a curt nod. Too late, Shawar noticed the burly Turk rushing to his side, who dragged him from his rearing horse.

"Traitor!" shrieked Shawar. "Guards, attack them!"

But Shawar's musicians, banner-carrier and guard were fleeing, galloping past the troops.

That afternoon, Caliph Aladid listened to the messenger report Saladin's arrest of Shawar. "Shawar was arrested? Interesting. Obviously, Shirkuh wishes to be my vizier. He is a capable man." He paced up and down the hall. "Tell him that when he delivers the head of Shawar, I shall appoint him my next vizier."

"But your highness," the royal advisor protested. "Shirkuh has attacked your representative. Is he to be rewarded?"

Aladid flipped his hand. "There is no reason to fear. The Syrians know that they dare not attempt to unseat me. And I like a man with initiative."

Shirkuh now became vizier, coming that much closer to the heart of the throne.

Nine weeks later, Shirkuh's plans plunged to oblivion. After grossly overeating at a banquet, he fell ill and died.

Saladin took his place.

Now, after Caliph Aladid, Saladin was the most powerful man in Egypt. He was thirty years old.

But almost immediately, Saladin had to deal with unrest. His forty thousand Nubian troops rebelled, and Saladin repressed the uprising mercilessly and bloodily.

The white troops—Arab, Turkomen, Armenian and others—also rose up against Saladin's policy of replacing the Fatimid generals with Syrian officers, and Saladin put down this rebellion as well.

Even as he did so, he faced trouble from the Christians.

Amalric joined forces with Byzantium, formerly an ally of Egypt, and launched a major attack on the port of Damietta.

But Saladin fought off his assault.

Now Saladin had demonstrated his great ability and power.

The Caliph of Egypt, Aladid, was a teenager who had little strength in the face of Saladin's growing might.

And Saladin intended to usurp the throne.

10

Tofostat

ALONGSIDE THE SILTY WATER, ARABS IN RAGGED HEADDRESSES urged along the stolid donkeys that pulled the barge past fields of rice and wheat.

Among the other passengers on board were the members of Rabbi Moshe's family.

Rabbi Moshe's third sister, Miriam, had remained behind in the West.

A few weeks earlier, Rabbi Moshe had turned to Rabbi David, his brother.

"I have decided that it would now be best to move to Fostat."

"Fostat?" Rabbi David said. "That ruined, burned-out city? Not even all the refugees who fled from there have returned."

"Yes, Fostat," said Rabbi Moshe, "and precisely because of what you say. Those refugees need a leader. And besides that, the rabbinic Jews are weak and the Karaites, who were always the richest Jews, are gaining more power and prestige.

"Cairo is the center of the Karaite movement. Most of the Jews there are Karaites. If there isn't a strong rabbinical leadership there, they will spread out across all of Egypt and into the neighboring countries."

Rabbi David sipped coffee from a cup decorated with a blue and red pattern.

"What about you, Rabbi David?"

Rabbi David compressed his lips. "Actually, this might be a good move for me. The Mediterranean is filled with hostile warships. Last year's naval blockade of Damietta by the Christians harmed a great many merchants. And that isn't even to mention the danger of pirates.

"As for Cairo, it is only one hundred and thirty miles from the ports on the Red Sea. I am told that many traders sail from there to India. And in Cairo, the business of imported gems is particularly successful because of the many officials of the palace and their harems."

"Trade with India?" Rabbi Moshe interrupted. "That means journeys away from home. You shall have to sail south on the Nile, and travel on caravans eastward across the desert to reach the Red Sea, where the ships come in from India and China. Are you and your wife prepared to make such a sacrifice?"

Rabbi David laughed easily. "Moshe, we decided after the death of our father that you and I would divide up the business of the family like Yissachar and Zevulun. You will learn, and with the help of G-d, I will provide the income."

"Very well, then," Rabbi Moshe replied. "But I charge you never to take untoward risks. Do not go on long, dangerous journeys."

Now the barge moved forward, a small wake disappearing into the heavy, greasy water.

At the shallow bank a crocodile lay motionless, its long snout agape, exposing uneven teeth. In its jaws, an Egyptian plover hopped about, pecking at the leeches and other small animals that clung to its teeth.

Another day of travel passed. Rabbi Moshe and his family now travelled with a caravan past cultivated fields and palm trees.

They passed through a village. Above the blue doors of the adobes were painted large drawings of an eye with an arrow piercing its pupil. This was to protect the house against the evil eye—reminiscent of the comment in the *Gemara*, "Do not say to the Satan, 'An arrow in your eye!'"

Storks were perched on the thatched roofs, and pigeons fluttered in the street.

Several young boys sat in the shade of a copse of palm trees, rocking back and forth and reciting verses from the Koran.

Passing the village, the caravan skirted an olive orchard. Beneath the trees with thin, twisting trunks were spread striped sheets. Three Arab farmers beat the branches with long rods, knocking down the ripe olives and barely glancing at the caravan.

Some miles later, the road led to a delta.

"Look!" someone called out.

Stretched across the breadth of the marshland was a shimmering movement of white and pink. Over a thousand flamingos were standing in the water, four feet tall on stick legs, with snake-like necks.

Later, Rabbi Moshe would write, in regard to the wonders of creation, "What is the path to loving and fearing G-d? When one gazes at His great and wondrous actions and creatures and sees in them His infinite wisdom, one immediately loves, praises, glorifies and acquires a great desire to know G-d. When one thinks of these matters, a great fear immediately falls on a person, and he knows that he is a small, lowly creature with a small capacity for knowledge in relation to G-d, Who is all-knowing." (*Hilchos Yesodei Hatorah* 2:2)

Eight days of travel passed before the company of travellers saw the walls of Cairo and the fortified gate of Bab Alfutuh, sixty feet high. On each side of the gate was a massive turret, from which a more slender minaret rose another sixty feet up. At the top of the minaret, a circle of eight white columns supported a balcony above which hung a globe and, on top of that, the half-moon symbol of Islam.

The gates of the royal city were closed to Rabbi Moshe and his family. Only the royal family, their entourage, soldiers and visitors of state could enter.

A merchant with whom Rabbi Moshe's party was travelling had been there once. "What a place of divine beauty!" He kissed his bunched fingers and opened them. "The Caliph, may he rule for a thousand years, had ordered Turkish pottery and Persian porcelain from me. Only the finest merchants were allowed to enter. We made our way down the Kasabah, the High Street, which runs through the length of Cairo.

"The street opened into a broad passageway. There were royal guards in shining uniforms on great steeds. Statesmen from other lands strode by, including ambassadors from Africa carrying white staffs and wrapped in white togas.

"Everywhere, soldiers and government officials were rushing about. Then there was a commotion from the side of the square. Surrounded by men on horseback, a carriage rolled by, led by white horses wearing purple plumes. 'Who is it?' I asked the merchant next to me, a Turk. He answered me, 'A member of the royal family!' Before I could say another word, the carriage rolled before us. All I could see of the person inside was the white sleeve that he allowed to hang out the side window. The Turk rushed up to the carriage and reverently kissed the sleeve, and then backed away."

The merchant wiped his brow. "I admit that in the exaltation of the moment, I did the same.

"What an immense square it was! 'Here,' the Turk told me, 'Caliph Aladid organizes military parades where more than ten thousand troops assemble.'

"And surrounding this parade ground were orchards and pleasure gardens.

"To my left was the Caliph's Eastern Palace, an immense building containing—would you believe it, my friend?—Four thousand rooms! The Caliph, may he rule for a thousand years, lives there with a retinue of over twenty thousand people: his wives and children, his personal servants and his many eunuchs.

"And that wasn't all!" the plump merchant continued volubly, adjusting his turban. "On my right side was another immense building, the Western Palace. This building was filled with visitors of state and yet more slaves and servants. And as for their wealth and magnificence—well, let me tell you just one little story that will illustrate."

They passed the length of the city. Soldiers were clustered about Bab Zuwayla, the southern gate.

As they continued travelling southward, the land was bare. There were encampments of impoverished people and urchins racing about in rags. Scattered across the plain were newly-built houses and mud-brick shacks. The crowds grew thicker, the huts more crowded.

Ahead, Rabbi Moshe saw a ruined city from which sprouted, like fresh mushrooms after a rain, new, white-washed buildings.

Within half an hour, they had arrived at Fostat. Amidst the swirling crowds of people were the ruins of a destroyed city. Everywhere, there were blackened hulks of buildings and lots upon which huge mounds of ruined bricks and charred wood were piled. The dust on the road was mixed with black particles of charcoal. Strewn across the roads and yards, they could see thousands of shattered remnants of the clay jars that, filled with naphtha, had a few years earlier turned the city of Fostat into an inferno.

They could even smell the ineradicable, pungent odor of smoke.

But new buildings were being constructed. The shells of the fourteen-story buildings were being rebuilt. Men with rags on long poles were scrubbing the blackened faces of the buildings clean.

Their guide brought them to a newly-built section of the city. A quarter of a mile away, the sparkling Nile was visible. A *dhow* sailed on the water.

A purple heron flew overhead, beating its wings slowly and heavily, like an ancient Egyptian argosy rowing its oars against the Nile.

"A phoenix!" exclaimed their guide. "How lucky! You shall have good fortune here."

11

In Fostat

A GROUP OF RABBIS WALKED INTO THE JEWISH MARKETPLACE. IN THE little shops, artisans made porcelain—"so fine and transparent," a Persian traveller wrote, "that a hand held outside a vase can be seen through it. They are decorated with colors whose shades change with the position of the object."

Rabbi Moshe stood in the midst of the rabbinical leaders of Fostat. To his right stood Rabbi Aharon Halevi, and to his left, the man in charge of distributing charity, Rabbi Chalphon.

"Friends," Rabbi Moshe called out, "we have received word that more of our brothers and sisters have been captured upon the seas and taken into captivity. After they were brought to Egypt, they were kidnapped by bandits and taken to Eretz Yisrael. The bandits are now demanding a great ransom. Now, my brothers, take a stand in this manner and gain a great reward from Heaven.

"Because this is an emergency, I have come to the market-place together with the most distinguished rabbinical scholars and leaders to encourage you to redeem the captives as the Torah commands us. 'The bridegroom must leave his chamber, and the bridegroom her wedding-chamber.' (*Yoel* 2:16) I urge all of you to contribute generously.

"May we see the fulfillment of the verse, 'Tell the imprisoned, 'Go out,' and to him in darkness, 'Be freed!' (*Yeshayahu* 49:9)" (*Igros Harambam, Shailat,* p. 67).

Day and night, Rabbi Moshe and the other leaders of Fostat circulated amidst the Jews of Fostat, raising funds to ransom the captives.

Rabbi Moshe summoned Rabbi Aharon Halevi and Rabbi Chalphon. "We cannot raise enough money ourselves to free these captives. I want you to travel across Egypt, to all the cities and towns of the plain—to Damira, Jorjer, Samanud, Damsis and Sumbat. Go to the elders of the community and to the commonfolk. Honor everyone and seek help from everyone. I shall give you a letter that will authorize you to raise funds and that will urge the communities to deliver the money into your hands."

"Rabbi Moshe, I myself am in poor circumstances," Rabbi Aharon replied. "But I will not hesitate to go—first, because you have asked me to do so, and second, because it is my responsibility to my fellow-Jews."

"I agree," echoed Rabbi Chalphon. "Any Jew is our fellow-Jew, even if we do not know him, even if he lives in a foreign land and speaks a foreign tongue. I too will not hesitate to wear myself out, for 'he who saves one Jewish life is considered to have saved the world.'" (based on *Igros Harambam, Shailat,* p. 68)

Rabbi Moshe sat down and wrote letters for the two *talmidei chachamim* to carry.

Rabbi Moshe also took an active role in countering the

activities of the Karaites. In most ways, the Karaite interpretation of the Torah was much more strict than that of the rabbis; for instance, according to the Karaites, even babies were obligated to fast on *Yom Kippur.* But in other ways, the Karaites were more lenient.

The unlearned rabbinic Jews were confused and swayed by the arguments of the Karaites.

At about this time, Rabbi Moshe finished the work that he called *Kitab Al Fara'id*—or, in Hebrew translation, *Sefer Hamitzvos.*

This, like his other writings, was meant to clarify the Torah for the masses of Jews as well as to delight the scholars.

The Sages of the *Gemara* had taught that there are six hundred and thirteen *mitzvos*: three hundred and sixty-five negative commandments and two hundred and forty-eight positive commandments. (*Makkos* 23b)

But exactly what were these commandments? The Sages were silent on that point.

In the eighth century, the Gaon Shimon Kairo elucidated the six hundred and thirteen *mitzvos* in his *Hilchos Gedolos,* and many great sages, such as Saadia Gaon and the philosopher and poet, Rabbi Shlomo ibn Gabirol, created compilations relying on his *sefer.* Many *paitanim*—poets—composed *azharos* (poems discussing the *mitzvos*) on this theme.

Rabbi Moshe disagreed on various points with these authorities, and he intended to compose a work that would combine simplicity with authority.

In his Introduction, Rabbi Moshe wrote, "I was seized with sorrow regarding a matter that has pained me for years. Regarding the counting of the *mitzvos*, people have imagined matters the depth of whose incorrectness I cannot even describe. Whoever has dealt in this field has followed in the footsteps of the author of the *Halachos Gedolos,* as though parroting his words.

"Similarly, whenever I heard the many *azharos* composed in Spain, I suffered, because I saw that this matter was so wide-spread. One cannot blame their authors, for they are poets and not rabbis, and they succeeded in their craft: the balance of speech and the beauty of the stanza. But in the content of the poem, they have been drawn after the author of the *Halachos Gedolos* and other, more recent rabbis."

Rabbi Moshe now wrote an overview of the six hundred and thirteen *mitzvos*, including various principles and rules of exegesis.

The work spread quickly throughout the entire Jewish world.

Rabbi Moshe had written *Sefer Hamitzvos* in Arabic so that the common man would understand it. But in those lands where Arabic was not the spoken language, *Sefer Hamitzvos* was incomprehensible.

Rabbi Moshe was too busy to translate his work into Hebrew, but he oversaw its translation by others.

It was perhaps at this time that Rabbi Moshe's wife passed away. There are those who say that she had given him a son and daughter and that these children too died.

Fostat had many unhygienic areas. An Arab physician, ibn Ridwan, described, "One of the practices of the people of Fostat is to throw into the streets and alleys everything that dies in their houses: cats, dogs and other domestic animals of that kind. They rot there, and this putrescence spreads through the air. Another of their habits is to throw into the Nile, whose water they drink, the remains and the corpses of their animals. Their latrines empty into the Nile and sometimes obstruct the flow of the water. They thus drink this putrid matter mixed with their water."

The germs spread by such unsanitary habits could cause disease and death.

But in truth, it is not known exactly when she died. Some

go so far as to doubt that Rabbi Moshe had been married before this time. Although he was already about thirty years old, it is possible that the difficulties of his wandering life had not allowed him to find a wife.

Rabbi Moshe became one of the leading rabbis of Fostat. He taught Torah and answered *halachic* questions that were sent to him from around the world.

Students came to learn under Rabbi Moshe from distant communities. One of these students was Rabbi Shlomo Hakohen from Yemen. Rabbi Shlomo Hakohen eventually had to return to his native land, but he never forgot the greatness of Rabbi Moshe. That is why, several years later, when the Jews of Yemen needed help, Rabbi Shlomo Hakohen was instrumental in eliciting Rabbi Moshe's help.

The synagogue of Fostat, called Knesiyat Ilshmiyin, followed the customs of Eretz Yisrael. It is said that Rabbi Moshe built a new synagogue that would follow his own, Spanish custom, *Nusach Bavel*. This synagogue was called Alirakiyin, and was also known as Beis Knesses Eliyahu Hanavi.

The Jewish-Egyptian historian, Sambori, wrote in his *Divrei Yosef* that this synagogue went up with miraculous swiftness, as a result of the pronunciation of G-d's Name.

At the top of the *heichal,* near the ceiling and covered by a *paroches,* was a *Sefer Torah* said to have been written by Ezra Hasofer. No one dared go up and bring it down, for there was a tradition that whoever entered the *heichal* to do so would not live out the year. However, it is said that it was this *Sefer Torah* that Rabbi Moshe used to determine the correct *mesorah.*

One day, Rabbi Moshe went to the dock of the Nile, accompanied by Rabbi Mishael. Rabbi Mishael was a highly learned man, one of the elders of Fostat. Here they might gain news about the captives with whose fate he was so concerned.

Heavy merchants' *dhows,* loaded with barrels and containers, were docked on the black-earthen banks. Along the length of the river were ramshackle buildings where merchandise was stored, and other buildings where shipwrights were constructing boats.

But there was no news today. With Rabbi Mishael Halevi, Rabbi Moshe returned to the city, passing the Market of the Lamps, where merchants sold luxurious items to wealthy government officials. Here hung a profusion of exotic items: elephant tusks from Zangebar and Abyssinian slippers that had the appearance of leopard skin.

"Rabbi Moshe."

"Yes, Rabbi Mishael?" Rabbi Moshe said.

"Shlomo Hamelech tells us that 'he who has found a wife has found goodness.' And our Sages teach that 'he who is without a wife is without completeness and without joy.'"

Rabbi Mishael looked into Rabbi Moshe's eyes.

"You know that I have an unmarried daughter." He paused. "Must I say anything more?"

About them, shopkeepers cried out and loaded donkeys were led down the street by barefoot boys.

"Rabbi Mishael," Rabbi Moshe said at last. "You honor me far more than I could have possibly wished for."

The older man put out his hands, and the two men shook hands warmly.

One day soon afterwards, red flags dotted with white stars hung out of windows of the houses in the Jewish quarter of Fostat. Underneath a wedding canopy made of a prayer shawl stood Rabbi Moshe and next to him his bride Jamilah (a common Arabic name meaning "beautiful").

Rabbi Moshe became fast friends with Rabbi Mishael's pious and brilliant son Uziel (his Arabic name was Abu Almaali). Eventually, Rabbi Uziel married Rabbi Moshe's sister.

For the rest of their lives, these two families were intimately involved with each other. Besides Rabbi Uziel, Rabbi Mishael had four other sons. Their names were Yeshayahu (Bonsur), Dosa (Abu Matzur, or Abu Mansur), Eliyahu (Abu Altahar) and Yekusiel (M'charam).

In 1171, Rabbi David took leave of his wife and brother, travelling southward along the Nile, past the green strips of irrigated land where papyrus plants grew in thick profusion. Beyond these were the endless expanses of arid, lifeless desert. In the Sudan, he passed through thin grassland and at the banks of the Nile, giant hippopotamuses wallowed and crocodiles basked in the sunshine.

Rabbi Moshe sent a letter of parting to his beloved brother:

"'May G-d be your trust and keep your foot from slipping.' (*Mishlei* 3:26) 'Peace, peace to the far and to the near, says Hashem.' (*Yeshayahu* 57:19) 'And you shall say, So may it always be for you, Peace to you and to your household peace.' (*Shmuel I* 25:6)

"The exalted G-d knows the pain and sorrow in my heart because of the departure of my dear and most beloved brother. May G-d save me by allowing no harm to come to you, and may we again be together in Fostat, with G-d's help.

"And I wish to let you know that I am doing very well." (*Igros Harambam, Shailat,* p. 76)

12

The Letter to Yemen

"UZIEL, MY SON."

"Yes, Father." Uziel was puzzled—and worried. His father, Rabbi Mishael, rarely came to see him.

Rabbi Uziel's wife entered with a silver salver. Setting down a glazed teapot and two glasses, she glided from the room.

Rabbi Uziel poured tea into the glasses, and the men sipped the peppermint tea.

"Uziel, now is the time for you to consider a position in the palace as a secretary."

"But Father, you know the position of rabbinic Jews," Rabbi Uziel checked himself. "What is happening, Father?"

Rabbi Mishael smiled slightly. "You have a quick wit, my son. Indeed, something is happening in Cairo.

"Last Friday, in the chief mosque, a Moslem from Mosul,

Iraq, was leading the prayer services. When he pronounced the blessings on the leaders of the Moslem people, he left out the name of Caliph Aladid."

"But that means revolution!" Rabbi Uziel thought a moment. "Obviously, Saladin is positioning the Sunni Moslems so that they will overthrow Caliph Aladid, the Shiite. If there is bloodshed, who knows how many Jews may die?" He looked urgently at his father. "What was Aladid's response?"

"There has been absolutely no response at all," Rabbi Mishael said.

"How is that possible?"

"There are rumors that Caliph Aladid is deathly ill."

"Although he is only twenty years old?"

"Yes. And besides that, his court is weak, and the people do not love him."

"But even if there is a revolution," Rabbi Uziel said, "how would that affect me?"

"Not only you," Rabbi Mishael said, "but, G-d willing, it will affect all the Jews for the good." He set down his glass of tea. "Caliph Aladid and his government have favored the Karaites over us rabbinic Jews."

"Yes, I know that too well," sighed Rabbi Uziel. "They identify with the Karaites because just as the Karaites claim to follow the authentic Torah without an oral tradition, the Shiites claim to follow the authentic Koran without any explanations."

"Correct," said his father. "But now, if Saladin becomes ruler of Egypt—as seems likely—the Sunnis will take power. And so they may decide to favor us over the Karaites."

"I see what you are saying. Now is the time to begin preparing to enter the service of the new government. You are always wise, Father. I shall immediately begin sending out feelers among the merchants and intellectuals I know who have connections with Saladin's forces."

The following Friday, the prayer-leader again omitted the prayer for Caliph Aladid. Moreover, he substituted a prayer for another caliph: Almustadi.

At almost the same time, Caliph Aladid died.

Saladin sent troops into the Eastern and Western Palaces. All members of Aladid's family were placed under house arrest, and the men separated from the women, so that there might be no more children born of the Fatimid line to claim the throne.

Saladin at last held power over Egypt. The rule of the Shiite Moslems was over, and the reign of the Sunni Moslems had begun.

But across the Red Sea, at the southern tip of Saudi Arabia, the Shiite Moslems still ruled. And under their oppression, the Jews of Yemen were suffering.

Rabbi Shlomo Hakohen, who had learned in Fostat under Rabbi Moshe, grieved in his heart as he walked along the dusty road to the synagogue. How long could a people suffer before they broke? What could give his people courage before they would cease to struggle and allow the pressure of the Moslems to wash them away?

In the shadowy synagogue, Rabbi Shlomo Hakohen stood before Rabbi Yaakov ben Nesanel Alfayumi, one of the leaders of the Yemenite Jews.

"What did you wish to see me about?" Rabbi Alfayumi spoke softly.

"We are suffering so much!" Rabbi Shlomo burst out. "We must have some hope—some consolation."

Rabbi Alfayumi replied in a soft whisper, "G-d is testing us. What do you propose, my son?"

"With all respect to you," Rabbi Shlomo said, "I met in Fostat a man whose Torah knowledge has no measure. I believe that he is the Torah leader of this generation. He risked his life to write his Letter on Apostasy, which saved the community of Morocco from despair. Please, Rabbi Alfayumi, if you write to him."

"Write to him?" Rabbi Alfayumi spoke as if to himself. "He is so far away. What would I write to Rabbi Moshe?"

"Everything!" Rabbi Shlomo burst out.

"If, as you say, he is such a great man." Rabbi Alfayumi's voice was low and hypnotic, his face hidden in the shadow of the colonnade. "Very well. I shall write to Rabbi Moshe. I shall tell him of the grief that has shattered our hearts. I shall tell him of the persecution that has broken our people, of the apostasy that is wearing us down, and of the false Messiah who is leading our people astray. I shall write everything there is to tell. And the merciful and compassionate G-d will direct matters as He sees fit."

He nodded at Rabbi Shlomo. Hurriedly, Rabbi Shlomo brought Rabbi Alfayumi a parchment, pen and inkwell.

Dipping the pen in the ink, Rabbi Alfayumi began to scratch the words of his letter on the page. "To the great light of Torah, Rabbi Moshe ben Maimon, may his light shine, I am writing to you regarding the condition of the Jews in Yemen on the recommendation of the fine young man."

In the *beis midrash* in Fostat Rabbi Moshe, held the letter in his hand. "Of the fine young man, Shlomo Hakohen, who learned under you in the city of Fostat."

As Rabbi Moshe read the letter, his face darkened.

The ruler of Yemen, Abd al-Nabi ibn Mahdi, was attempting to force the Jews to convert to Islam.

He was being helped by an apostate Jew who preached to the Jews that the coming of Mohammed and Islam had been predicted in the Torah. And Jews were beginning to doubt the eternal veracity of the Torah.

And another Jew, who had at first declared himself to be a messenger of the Mashiach, now said that he was the Mashiach himself.

This man was known to be pious and learned, and he had apparently brought about a number of miracles. Many Jews and Moslems wandered after him in the hill country and entered the towns and villages to proclaim his greatness, telling how he revived the dead. They fasted, prayed and gave away all they had to the poor, as they awaited the day that G-d would transport them to the Promised Land.

Rabbi Moshe called his wife into the room. "I have made a hard decision," he said.

She looked at him with a question in her eyes.

Rabbi Moshe told her about the letter he had received. "In order to help the Jews of Yemen, I shall have to reply to this letter in a clear manner that everyone will understand—man, woman and child. That means that I will have to use such strong language about Islam that if my letter falls into the hands of the Moslems, my life may be endangered."

"Only you can make that decision, my husband."

Rabbi Moshe sighed. "I am very much afraid. But for the sake of saving a community of Jews, I am willing to undergo that risk." (*Igros Harambam, Shailat,* p. 167)

Deep into the night, Rabbi Moshe wrote. The brass lantern on the wall cast a small, golden light onto the parchment that he filled with elegant letters. The rooster in a nearby court-yard was crowing by the time Rabbi Maimon signed the letter and laid down his pen.

The next day, a trusted agent was carrying the letter beneath his robe on a caravan that would take him to the Red Sea, where he would sail southward to Yemen.

Two weeks later, Rabbi Yaakov ben Nesanel Alfayumi accepted the heavy envelope with trembling hands. Carrying it to his private study, he tore open the envelope and took out the sheets. He sat down by the window, where the light was clear, and began to read.

"I am the smallest of the small of the rabbis of Spain, whose glory was dragged down into exile," Rabbi Moshe began his letter. "I always am up late at night studying, yet I have not attained the wisdom of my forefathers, for I have met with evil, difficult days and had no tranquility. We have groaned and had no peace. How may the *halachah* be clear to a person who has wandered from city to city and from country to country."

Rabbi Moshe began by discussing the persecution campaign of the Yemenite government.

"In regard to the ruler of Yemen, who has declared a campaign of apostasy against the Jews and forced all the Jews in Yemen to become Moslems, this news has torn me apart and has upset our entire community.

"Such a matter should not decrease one's faith in G-d, in His Torah and in Moshe His servant. There is no doubt that these are the birthpangs of the Mashiach that our Sages prayed that they not be forced to experience.

"You have said that some Jews have assimilated and converted, and others have not. This has already been predicted by Daniel. He was told by G-d that when the exile would be long and we would suffer many sorrows, many people would be weakened in their religiosity. Doubt would enter their hearts, and they would be led astray.

"After this, Daniel explained that the wise men who would stand up to the sorrows and remain faithful in G-d and to His servant Moshe would suffer even more, until doubt would enter the heart of some of them as well, and they too would be led astray. Only a small number would remain pure.

"Now, my brothers, you should all listen carefully to what I tell you. Teach it to the young people and the children, in order to strengthen your faith and be strong in the truth: We have the true Torah that was given to us by the greatest of all prophets, with which G-d separated us from all other peoples—not because we were fit for it, but out of His love for us.

"He has made us special by giving us its *mitzvos* and laws, so that our superiority is clear insofar as we have the Torah.

"We were promised by G-d via Yeshayahu that whoever tries to overcome our Torah, whether by force or by argument, will be vanquished: 'Every weapon made against you will not succeed, and whatever tongue rises against you shall be condemned.' (Yeshayahu 54:17)

"The desire of the Nazarene and Mohammed was to make their religions similar to the Torah of Hashem. But the difference between our Torah and the teachings that are similar to it is like the difference between a living man who speaks and a statue. This state of affairs was also revealed by G-d via Daniel.

"There has never been a time that did not have a new persecution and trouble; and afterwards, G-d has always removed it.

"Know, my brothers, that the evil Nevuchadnezzar forced everyone to serve idols. Only Chananiah, Mishael and Azariah were saved from this decree. Yet afterwards, G-d destroyed Nevuchadnezzar and his law, and the truth returned to its place.

"The same occurred during the second Beis Hamikdash, when the evil Greeks pronounced terrible decrees of persecution against the Jews in order to wipe out the knowledge of Torah. They forced Jews to desecrate *Shabbos*, not circumcise their children and to write on their clothing and carve on the horns of their cows that they have no portion in the G-d of Israel. This continued for fifty-two years. And then G-d destroyed their kingdom and laws altogether.

"G-d already told Yaakov Avinu that even though other nations may subjugate the Jews, the Jews will always remain.

"He promised that He will not reject us all, even if we rebel and transgress His *mitzvos*.

"Rely on these verses, my brothers. Do not be frightened

by the constant persecutions and power of our enemies, and by the weakness of our people. This is all meant to test and to purify us, until only the pious, G-d-fearing Jews are left.

"Therefore, my brothers, all Jews spread across the world, you must encourage each other—the great encouraging the small, the leaders encouraging the masses. Agree without any question that G-d is uniquely One, that Moshe is the greatest of all prophets, that the Torah from beginning to end is the word of G-d to Moshe, that it will never be exchanged, and that no other religion will ever be given by G-d. Remember the giving of the Torah on Mount Sinai and teach it to your children. This is the nub of our religion.

"Stand fast in your commitment and your faith, my brothers. Strengthen your hearts and hope to G-d."

Rabbi Moshe turned his attention to the Jewish apostate who was enticing the Jews to believe that Islam had taken the place of the Torah.

"You have written of the evildoer who interprets various verses in *Tanach* as referring to Mohammed.

"These are ridiculously weak proofs that even the evildoers themselves do not believe to be true.

"They claim that the Jews revised the Torah and erased Mohammed's name from it. They have found no stronger argument, even though it is absolutely contemptible and weak, even in the eyes of the common man, since we possess ancient copies of translations of the Torah into other languages hundreds of years before the coming of Mohammed."

And Rabbi Moshe added a word of warning about the Karaites, whose presence had been so harmful in Egypt.

"Just as there is nothing added or lacking in the written Torah, so is it in the Oral Torah. Be on your guard against the Karaites, may they quickly disappear, for they can be worse than apostasy.

"Egypt is a land of wise men and their students and study

halls, so the Karaites' words are rebutted, and we speak of their error and falsehood and emptiness at every opportunity. But you are in the far-flung outreaches where your wise and powerful men in Torah and good deeds are few, may G-d increase your number. If one Karaite sneaks in among you, he will destroy everything and ruin the faith of the young. So take care."

Many Jews in Yemen sought solace in determining the time that the Mashiach would come, and Rabbi Moshe now spoke of that.

"You have mentioned the investigation of the time of the coming of the Mashiach.

"It is impossible to know the date of his coming exactly, as Daniel has said. But even if people have predicted wrongly, Daniel admonished us not to let doubt enter our hearts. The more the Mashiach delays, the more must we anticipate him.

"My brothers, be strong, all of you who have faith in G-d. Encourage one another and have a strong faith in this anticipated one, may he soon be revealed.

"Know that G-d has already told us through Yeshayahu that, because our exile shall be so long and great, many of us will think that G-d has abandoned us, Heaven forbid. But He said that He will never set us aside.

"As to the time—it has been explained in the words of Daniel and Yeshayahu and the statements of our Sages that the Mashiach will come when the kingdom of Rome and of the Arabs will spread out, as the situation is today. Daniel talked of the coming of the Mashiach directly after he spoke of the kingship of Ishmael and the rising of Mohammed. Yeshayahu also explained that the proof of the coming of the Mashiach is the rising of Mohammed. These are matters that are obvious from the simple meaning of the verses.

"The exact true time is not known.

"But I have a wonderful tradition that I received from my

father and from my grandfather, who received it from their fathers and grandfathers, back to the beginning of our exile from Jerusalem.

"Balaam prophesied, 'At this time shall it be said to Yaakov and to Yisrael, What has G-d wrought?' This contains a secret. 2486 years passed from the six days of creation to the time of Balaam's prophecy. Prophecy will return to Israel after the same number of years. Then the prophets will say, 'What has G-d wrought?' According to this explanation of the verse, prophecy will return to Israel 2486 years after that prophecy, in the year 4972 (1211). There is no question that the return of prophecy to Israel precedes the Mashiach. This is the most true of all predictions regarding the end.

"We were told that this is true, but warned not to make the date known so that people should not know how late it is.

"And now we have told you. And G-d knows the truth."

Obviously, the Mashiach did not come in 1211. It may be relevant to note, however, that it was approximately at that time that the *Kabbalah* began to be revealed.

Rabbi Moshe now dealt with the Jews who were following the self-proclaimed Mashiach.

"You have told me about a man in the cities of Yemen who claims to be the Mashiach. By my life, I am not impressed by him or by those drawn after him. About him I am not surprised—he is insane without a doubt, and there is nothing shameful about a man who is ill. As for his followers, because of their difficult situation and their misunderstanding about how great the Mashiach will be, they have believed this.

"But I am surprised at you, Rabbi Alfayumi, you who are a student of the Torah, thinking that this might be true.

"Do you not know, my brother, that the Mashiach is a very great prophet, greater than all the prophets after Moshe Rabbeinu? How surprising is your statement that this man is known for his fear of sin and that he has some wisdom—is this what defines the Mashiach of G-d?

"The Mashiach will arise in the land of Israel and there he will begin to be revealed. He will not be known at all before he is revealed.

"When he appears, G-d will distress all the kings of the earth when they hear of him. They will lose their kingdoms and will be unable to stand against him. They will be amazed at the signs and wonders and will be silent.

"He will put to death whoever it pleases him to do so, and no one will be saved from his hand. However, the end of war from east to west will not occur at the beginning of his revelation, but after the War of Gog, as Yechezkiel explained.

"If this man had spoken wilfully, he would be deserving of death. But I believe, and it is true, that he is insane and imagining things.

"I offer you the following good advice. Imprison him for a while and make it known to everyone, including the gentiles, that he is not sane. Afterwards, free him. In this way, you will save him, for when the gentiles hear his words, they will laugh at him and consider him mad, as he is. And you will save yourselves from the evil of the gentiles.

"But if you allow the matter to rest until the gentiles learn of it, they will kill him and perhaps anger will come upon you because of him."

Now Rabbi Moshe ended his letter with words of consolation and hope.

"Know, my brothers, that G-d has led us on a hard path with this nation of Ishmael, which does so much to torment us and to create laws to persecute us. There has not stood against Israel a nation more evil, none that has done so much to cast us down, subjugate us and treat us with hatred.

"We who suffer what a person cannot bear have accustomed ourselves, both great and small, to tolerate their subjugation. But with all this, we suffer their evil outbreaks all the time. As much as we bear it in order to be with them in peace, they incite against us war and the sword. And how much more, if we foolishly irritate them, then we are giving ourselves over to death.

"The Creator of the world will in His compassion, remember us and you. He will gather the exiles of His portion to gaze at the sweetness of G-d and to visit His Beis Hamikdash. He will bring us out of the valley of the shadow of death. He will remove the veil from our eyes and the darkness from our hearts, and establish for us the verse, 'The nation that walks in darkness saw great light, light shall dwell upon those who dwell in a land of the shadow of death.' (*Yeshayahu* 9:1) May He bring darkness in His wrath and anger upon all those who rise up against us, and may He illuminate our darkness, as He has promised: 'Behold, the darkness shall cover the land and clouds over the nations, and upon you shall Hashem shine.' (*Ibid.* 60:2)

"I request that you send this letter to every community to strengthen their faith. Read it to the public and individuals so that you may be one of those who does good for the masses. But be extremely careful to guard yourself from any evil [Jew] so that he does not reveal it to the gentiles, G-d save us from what may result then.

"I have sent out another copy of the letter to someone else. And our Sages, who are in the place of the prophets, have already promised us, 'Messengers of a *mitzvah* are not harmed.' (*Pesachim* 8:33) And there is no *mitzvah* greater than this.

"Peace upon Israel. Amen."

In mud and lime huts, families gathered together to hear the letter; in the synagogues lined with cushions and mats of goat hide; in courtyards where pomegranate trees grew. Weavers and carpenters, engravers and bookbinders, millers and calligraphers all listened to Rabbi Moshe's words and took comfort. "Rabbi Moshe says that our troubles and sorrows

136

have been spoken of by the prophets. It is not true that G-d has forgotten us. Let us be strong in our faith."

Learned Jews travelled throughout the communities of Yemen, gathering Jews and reading the letter to them.

Women met at each other's homes, embroidering and sewing. From the oven came the scent of bread made of grain and legume flour. "I must admit that I had been troubled by the proofs brought by the apostate when he spoke here last year. But Rabbi Moshe has shown his arguments to be so foolish!"

Men came home on *Shabbos* eve to their wives and daughters, who greeted them with fragrant boughs in their hands. They discussed Rabbi Moshe's words at the *Shabbos* meal. "Listen to what Rabbi Moshe says about the founders of Christianity and Islam. Yes, he is right! Why should we be ashamed before them? It is our Torah that is true!"

In the synagogue, the men sat drinking aromatic coffee from a silver urn, their sidelocks tightly curled. "Did you hear what Rabbi Moshe said about the man who claims that he is the Mashiach? He is just a madman!"

Although the persecutions continued and the apostate continued his activities, the Jews no longer questioned their faith.

Various translations were made of this letter into Hebrew. One of the translators, Rabbi Nachum Maaravi, called it *Petach Tikvah: The Gateway of Hope*; and thus has it been called to this day.

In one town, a scholar shook his head over the letter. "There is a contradiction here," he said. "In his *Pirush Hamishnayos*, Rabbi Moshe writes that one should be committed to keeping *mitzvos* regardless of one's desire for reward or fear of punishment. Yet here he speaks of nothing else but reward and punishment."

Another scholar replied, "You don't understand. In his

Commentary, Rabbi Moshe spoke to the man who learns Torah and who has developed his mind and maturity. This letter is meant for the masses. Rabbi Moshe has written here in a style that will appeal to the mind of the simplest Jew. When a person is more sophisticated, one desires more nuanced arguments. But this letter is not meant to provide intellectual delight. It is meant to save our communities."

Rabbi Moshe's letter did not prevent the activities of the false Mashiach. Rabbi Moshe wrote later in a letter to the rabbis of Marseilles, "After a year, this man was caught, and all of his followers fled.

"The Arab king who had captured him told him, 'What have you done?'

"He replied, 'I have done that which is true, and have acted according to the word of G-d.'

"The king said to him, 'What sign do you have?'

"He replied, 'Cut off my head, and I shall live.'

"Immediately, the king told him, 'There is no greater sign than this. If you do this, certainly I and everyone will believe and know that our Moslem forefathers taught us falsehood.'

"Immediately, they killed that poor person, may his death be an atonement for him and for all of Israel.

"The Jews were punished in most areas with a monetary fine.

"And to this day, there are those who lack understanding who say that he will be resurrected." (*Igros Harambam, Shailat*, p. 189)

Two years passed. In 1174, Saladin's brother, Turan Shah, conquered Yemen. He nullified the decrees of persecution and forced apostasy against the Jews. Just as Rabbi Moshe had predicted in his letter, the Jews' powerful oppressors fell in an instant. Now they could again practice their Judaism openly. Besides this, many of the terrible conditions that had reduced them to poverty were removed.

Meanwhile, in Damascus, Sultan Nureldin died.

Saladin, though ruler of much of the Middle East, had never been more than the viceroy of Nureldin. Would he now be able to take Nureldin's crown?

Two months later, Amalric, thirty-eight-year-old leader of the Christians, died of dysentery.

Two immensely powerful military forces were now essentially lacking leadership.

Swiftly, Saladin travelled up to Syria with his army. In a short time, he defeated his rivals and ruled over all of Syria (except for Aleppo), Egypt and Yemen.

Saladin remained in Syria for two more years.

Then, in 1176, he returned to Cairo as the mightiest ruler of the Moslem empire.

One morning, Rabbi Moshe rode up the road from Fostat to Cairo. To his left, on top of a gently sloping hill, thousands of workers were swarming, building a massive stone wall.

Rabbi Moshe turned to Rabbi Uziel. "What is that construction?"

"That, Rabbi Moshe—excuse me." Rabbi Uziel trailed off. "I meant to say, Chief Rabbi! But it's just that you've only been recently installed, and I've been used . . . That will be what is called the Citadel. The workers are Christian prisoners. Sultan Saladin is building his palace there."

"And the Eastern Palace?"

"Well, the Sultan is stationed there now, of course. But he is also using it to quarter his officers. It is all part of his plan to destroy the way that Caliph Aladid ruled, distant from the people."

They said no more until they arrived at Bab Zuwayla, the southern gate of Cairo. Five years previously, when Rabbi Moshe had first come to Fostat, this gate had been sealed to all but the privileged members of Caliph Aladid's government and visitors of state.

Now crowds of merchants were flowing through.

Rabbi Moshe and his entourage rode along the Kasabah, Cairo's main street. From outside the city walls, the massive bulk of the Eastern Palace had risen like a mountain. But here, all that Rabbi Moshe saw as they approached the palace was the high wall before it.

On the palace grounds, Rabbi Moshe passed through a series of twelve pavilions. In one of them sat a golden throne that took up the width of the room, engraved with scenes of riders racing their horses. A balustrade of golden latticework surrounded the throne, and behind it were steps of silver. But on the throne had been hurriedly cast the rough cloth of a military tent. Three officers stood in a corner of the room, and soldiers marched through, their shoes leaving tracks on the marble floor.

Rabbi Moshe and his entourage passed into an outdoor court surrounded by colonnaded porticoes, paved with marble of various colors and set off with gold. In the center of the courtyard, a fountain poured water into canals and pools. The pipes that brought the water to the fountain were made of gold and silver.

Beautiful songbirds from all corners of the Orient sang in the tree branches.

But piles of trash had been cast into the corners of the courtyard.

At last, they arrived at the Eastern Palace itself.

Again, they passed through magnificent rooms. Finally, they entered a room through the middle of which hung a curtain strewn with figures of animals, birds and people, aflame with hundreds of rubies, emeralds and other precious stones.

It was in this room that Caliph Aladid used to receive his visitors, his face covered by a veil.

Now soldiers and officers filled the room. Sultan Saladin

sat upon the golden throne dressed in his military uniform.

An adjutant approached Rabbi Moshe's company and asked them their business.

After the many merchants and statesmen had stood before him, came Rabbi Moshe's turn before the Sultan.

The adjutant announced, "Rabbi Moshe ben Maimon, Chief Rabbi of the Jews of Fostat and Cairo."

Saladin gazed down at Rabbi Moshe. He was younger than Rabbi Moshe, but he had spent his life in adventure and battle. He was a ruler and he looked out with confidence and power. "Your brother-in-law Abu Almaali [Rabbi Uziel's Arabic name] is the secretary to my mother. He has spoken to me upon your behalf. What is your desire, Rabbi Moshe?"

"Sultan Saladin," Rabbi Maimon replied, "may you rule forever in glory and in victory. All the Jews of Egypt rejoice in your power and victory.

"I have come to speak for my fellow Jews in Yemen. There, most gracious sultan, you have torn away the unjust might of the Shiite rulers and replaced it with your munificent rule. Under the Shiites, the Jews of Yemen were subjected to harsh and evil decrees of apostasy. And they were also subjected to great hardship because of the many unfair taxes that the previous government had placed upon them, simply because they are Jewish. Many of the decrees are still in effect.

"On their behalf, I ask you to remove these unfair decrees.

"All the Jews of Yemen pray to Heaven for your continued might and success, and shall accept with gratefulness and loyalty the mercy that I am confident you shall show them."

"Very well," Saladin replied. "I shall have my viceroys recall these decrees that you speak of."

"You are most gracious, your highness."

On the street, merchants were setting up shops in the great square where once only dignitaries had walked. In one quarter of the square, a cloud of fine dust rose as workmen smashed an ashlar wall. The planned, symmetrical city was losing its character of royal capital. Already, it was beginning to resemble a metropolis.

On the path back to Fostat, Rabbi Yitzchak ben Rabbi Sasson turned to Rabbi Moshe. "Today, Rabbi Moshe, I have seen with my own eyes that you are a great lover of Israel. Everything that you do is motivated for the sake of the Torah and for the sake of all Jews."

13

Contra Karaite

RABBI MOSHE HAD BEEN SADDENED TO TAKE LEAVE OF HIS BROTHER. Rabbi David was setting out again to engage in his gem business.

"Take care," Rabbi Moshe had said. "Do not go farther than the Sudanese coast. There you will meet the merchants who have sailed to India and China. Trade with them and return home in safety."

Now Rabbi Moshe held in his hand a letter that his brother had written him.

"To my beloved brother, Rabbi Moshe ben Rabbi Maimon, from your brother David, who is longing for you—may G-d unite us in His grace under the most happy circumstances.

"I am writing you this letter from Aydhab, the Sudanese port. I am well, but my mind is much troubled. I walk about the bazaar, and I hardly know where I am.

"I first arrived in Kus, a city on the Nile. From here, caravans travel for seven days. I and my friend were separated from the caravan, and we decided to travel by ourselves to Aydhab. No one has ever dared to embark on such a disastrous undertaking alone across the desert. I myself did it only because of my complete ignorance.

"But G-d saved us after many frightful encounters, which would lead me too far afield to mention here. As soon as we were in the desert, we regretted what we had done, but the matter was already out of our hands. However, G-d wished that we be saved.

"We finally arrived in Aydhab safely with all our belongings. While we were unloading our things at the city gate, the caravan arrived. Their passengers had been robbed, including ibn Alrashidi—some had been wounded, and some had died of thirst.

"We had preceded the caravan by only a small distance. We had been saved from the fate of robbery only because we had taken upon ourselves those frightful experiences of leaving the caravan.

"All day long I imagine how you must feel, having heard that ibn Alrashidi, the gift of G-d, was robbed, and thinking that I was together with him. Then G-d comes between me and my reason.

"To make a long story short, when I arrived in Aydhab, I found that no imports had arrived, and I found nothing to buy except indigo.

"I thought about how much I had endured in the desert yet been saved. So it appeared to me that it would be a comparatively easy matter to set sail."

Rabbi Moshe creased his brow. This was precisely what he had told his brother not to do!

"I will be sailing on the Malabar Sea . . . Despite this bad news, do not worry. He Who saved me from the desert will save me while I am on the sea.

"Please calm the heart of the little one, my wife, and her sister. Do not frighten them and do not let them despair, for 'crying to G-d over what has passed is a vain prayer.' (*Berachos* 9:3)

"I am doing all this in order to help support you, even though you have never obligated me to do so.

"Be steadfast. G-d will replace your losses and bring me back to you.

"At any rate, that which is done is done.

"I am sure that this letter will reach you at a time when I, with G-d's help, will have already sailed most of the way. 'But the counsel of G-d shall stand.' (*Mishlei* 19:21)

". . . Written on the twenty-second of *Iyar*, while the express caravan is on the point of leaving."

(This letter is found in S.D. Goitein's *The Indian Traders*, pp. 209-211.)

There was a knock at the door. Rabbi Moshe's mind was still on the letter. He had told David not to set sail! May G-d have mercy.

"Yes?"

It was his wife.

Seeing his worried face, she withdrew. "I am sorry. I shall ask Uziel to return later."

Rabbi Moshe shook his head slightly and smiled at his wife. "I am coming."

In the courtyard, under a thin, blue sky, Rabbi Uziel was smiling. He sang out in the Aramaic of the *Kaddish,* "May the Mashiach arrive in your lifetime and in your days and in the lifetime of Rabbi Moshe ben Maimon!"

Rabbi Moshe smiled at Rabbi Uziel's good spirits. "What are you saying, Uziel? Have you appointed me as the new Exilarch?"

It was the custom that on the day that a man became the

new Exilarch, he would be referred to this way in the *Kaddish.*

Rabbi Uziel replied, "The *beis din* has just received a letter from the Jews of Yemen that Saladin has repealed the terrible laws against them."

"May the compassionate G-d be praised."

"And in thanks to you, they are now including you in their *Kaddish*!"

"Really! It is an honor that I hope I can begin to earn."

The two men stepped out of the courtyard and walked toward the *beis midrash.* A small boy hurried by, carrying a straw mat on which lay half a dozen small quails, their feet trussed with palm leaves.

They passed a side street where two women stood gazing at a placard that had been pasted to a wall.

"Look at this notice!" said one of the women, dressed in a light blue robe. "It's an utter disgrace!"

"I've already heard what that placard says," the other woman replied, "and I agree with it."

"You what!" exclaimed the first woman. "Don't you know that when this placard says 'heretics,' it's referring to us Karaites? Are you being tempted by the words of the rabbinic Jews?"

"I don't know about that. But I heard a rabbi speak at the synagogue, and—"

"Don't you know how those clever rabbis can interpret anything to make it come out their way? It is only our teachers, basing themselves on the great founder of our faith, Anan, who teach the Torah correctly."

"But the rabbi in the synagogue was pointing out that Anan too had to interpret things in the Torah. And our teachers in every generation over the last four hundred years keep changing and adding things. Doesn't that mean that we are interpreting, too?"

"Well, of course, the Torah must be understood correctly," the first woman said. "But we don't interpret according to made-up rabbinical rules. We interpret according to G-d's intent."

"I don't understand that either. The rabbinic Jews light candles on *erev Shabbos* and eat warm food. But we have to sit in the darkness and eat cold food. On *Shabbos* morning, they go to the synagogue and when they come home, they sing *zemiros*. But we stay at home and recite *selichos*.

"The rabbinic Jews allow a fire to be lit on *Shabbos* to help a childbearing woman. But we won't light a fire, even if the woman will die.

"The rabbinic Jews allow sick people to go to the doctor. But because the verse says, 'I am Hashem Who heals you' (*Shemos* 15:26), Anan said that we can never go to the doctor.

"It doesn't make any sense!"

"Ever since that Moshe ben Maimon has come to Fostat," the first woman exclaimed bitterly, he has done nothing but confuse the minds of the most simple among us."

"Well, you can call me simple," her friend retorted, "but I'll tell you one thing. I've decided that Rabbi Moshe is right. And not only that, I've persuaded my husband as well."

"What? I don't believe it. You're going to join that—that cult?"

"Call it what you want. I'm going to be raising my children as rabbinic Jews."

"Oh! What has that man done to our friendship?"

Meanwhile, Rabbi Moshe sat in his study, writing a work that would serve as the next step after his *Pirush Hamishnayos* and *Sefer Hamitzvos*. In this work, he would further clarify the *mitzvos* so that even a person unable to study the sources would be able to understand them.

Rabbi Moshe was surrounded by a coterie of *talmidei chachamim*. But about him, in an age of confusion about

147

halachah, when the level of scholarship was low, the Torah was being largely unlearned, and the Jewish people were bereft of knowledge.

Most of Rabbi Moshe's works were written in a simple style, so that the common man could understand them.

Never once did Rabbi Moshe permit himself the luxury of writing a line at the expense of being understood by his intended audience.

(Even his later and sophisticated philosophical writings were written solely to instruct students of philosophy.)

In later generations, Rabbi Moshe was praised for his "golden pen." It would have been possible for him to turn every simple sentence into a fountain of ideas. But he wrote so that his every idea might be clearly followed. Nevertheless, he did not sacrifice the "Fountain of Ideas." They are all there in the judicious choice of words, in the turn of phrase, in the arrangement of his arguments. For all generations afterwards, students would plumb the depths of his words and find them a virtually inexhaustible source of treasures.

Meanwhile, on the battlefield, the Christians again invaded the Holy Land and threatened to attack Syria. Saladin left Egypt to lead his army. After subduing the Christians, he returned to Damascus, Syria as his power base.

And in Cairo, Saladin's vizier Alfadil became the virtual ruler of Egypt.

14

Transition

THERE ARE MANY EPISODES IN RABBI MOSHE'S LIFE WHOSE BARE
description alone is known. Rabbi Moshe wrote once in a
letter, "There have occurred to me many bare sorrows in the
land of Egypt: illnesses, loss of money and informers who
sought to kill me."

There are as well episodes in Rabbi Moshe's personal life
whose content is known, but which cannot be communicat-
ed. So filled are they with exquisite feeling, of gladness or
sorrow, that they are ineffable.

Rabbi Moshe continued in his letter, "And then there
occurred the great evil that overcame me finally, the greatest
evil of any that has happened to me since the day of my
existence."

Who had brought the sorrowful news back to Rabbi
Moshe? Had it been a messenger carrying post from the ports

149

of the Sudan? Perhaps it had been a merchant who had heard gossip passing upon the docks of Aydhab, or a broker who had dealt with Rabbi David. "This great evil was the passing away of my brother, the righteous man, of blessed memory, who drowned in the Indian Ocean. He drowned holding a great deal of money belonging to me, to him and to others. He left behind a small daughter and her widow, who are living with me."

The death of his brother broke Rabbi Moshe's spirit. "For about a year from the day that the evil report arrived, I remained lying in bed. I suffered a skin disease, fever and a profoundly suffering heart, and I was almost lost."

Rabbi Moshe grieved, "He was like a son to me, growing up on my knees. He was my brother. He was my student." And Rabbi Moshe praised his brother, "He had a quick understanding of the Talmud and understood its details very well.

"I had no joy except in seeing him," Rabbi Moshe lamented. "My joy has passed and gone to eternal life, leaving me dismayed in a foreign land. Whenever I gaze upon his handwriting or one of his manuscripts, my heart turns within me and my pain is reawakened. 'I shall descend to the grave, my son, in mourning.' (*Beraishis* 37:35)

"If not for the Torah which is my delight," Rabbi Moshe concluded, "and the words of wisdom in which I forget my pain, I would have been lost in my poverty."

A year passed. Rabbi Moshe walked through the streets of Fostat. Little brass chimes rang in the cool, dusty wind. Overhead the sky seemed new and wet, with a blue, silky sheen. Rabbi Moshe pulled his white robe about him. He was more gaunt now, and weary. He entered the gate of his home, holding his *tallis* bag against his chest.

In the anteroom, six Jews, men and women, were waiting to see him. One of the women held a red-faced, squealing baby.

Rabbi Moshe passed into the next room. "I'll see the baby first."

An old man with a bowed posture rose up angrily. "Rabbi Moshe, I was here before this woman!"

Rabbi Moshe put his *tallis* bag onto a shelf. "Her child is in pain. Please sit down patiently. I shall see you shortly."

The woman stepped forward into Rabbi Moshe's examining room, which had once been his living room.

She handed the infant to Rabbi Moshe, her black eyes large above her veil.

After Rabbi Moshe had recovered from his grief over his brother's death, one of the rabbis had offered him a salary as chief rabbi.

"You are no longer supported by your brother," the rabbi had pointed out. "In addition, now you have to support his widow and daughter, as well as repay the debts he incurred. If you give your time to the citizens of Cairo to be chief rabbi, you should be reimbursed—"

"Please, no more," Rabbi Moshe interrupted. "Have you not read what I wrote about this in my commentary on *Pirkei Avos*?" He lifted a manuscript down from the shelf and flipped through the pages.

The rabbi took the manuscript from Rabbi Moshe's hands and turned it around so that it faced him. "Rabbi Tzadok said," he recited aloud, "'Do not make the Torah a spade with which to dig.' That's the quote from *Pirkei Avos*."

"Go on," Rabbi Moshe waved a hand. "Read my commentary now."

"Do not regard the Torah as a tool to make a living," the rabbi read. "Whoever has enjoyment in this world from the honor of the Torah removes his life from the World to Come. People have mistranslated this clear language of the *Mishneh* and cast it behind their backs. They assigned fixed taxes to individuals and communities and led people to believe with

151

total foolishness that it is an obligation to help sages and the students, people whose Torah is their occupation.

"'But this is all an error,'" the rabbi continued to read, "'and there does not exist in the Torah or in the words of the Sages anything that will justify this.

"'When we examine the words of the Sages, we will not find that they asked people for money. They didn't receive money for the great, important *yeshivos,* nor for the Exilarchs, nor for the judges, nor for the teachers, nor for any of the Torah leaders, nor for any other person. We will find that in every generation there was both abject poverty and incredible wealth.

"'They saw that taking money is a desecration of G-d's Name in the eyes of the masses, for they will consider the Torah as just another occupation.'"

Three months had passed since that time. Now Rabbi Moshe looked into the infant's eyes. In his youth, he had learned medicine from his father and from the physicians of Morocco. Now he would apply his abilities to earn a living.

"The child is colicky," Rabbi Moshe said. "Give him warm barley gruel sweetened with date honey. If he is not better, come back to me."

"Thank you," the woman murmured.

She scooped the child up into her left hand. With her right hand, she reached into the fold of her voluminous robe and cast a few coins onto the ledge. "Is that enough?"

Rabbi Moshe glanced down at the coins. They were the meanest coins, barely worth a few handfuls of flour.

"I'm sorry," the woman said. "My husband is a dyer, and we have many children, G-d protect them. If the payment is not sufficient—"

"No, it is enough," Rabbi Moshe said. "Don't forget to return if the crying doesn't stop."

The woman stepped out. Rabbi Moshe stood at the door

and motioned to the old, bowed man to enter. He wore a dirty, frayed robe. He too would pay no more than a few small coins.

In the afternoon, Rabbi Moshe walked into the street. A Jew from North Africa passed by and nodded his head in respect—one of Rabbi Moshe's students. Farther down the street, he passed a Spanish Jew. This man had learned with Rabbi Moshe the previous year. Now his wife and children had followed after him, and he earned a living as a silversmith.

A group of young students from Arabia passed by. They too were students, but Rabbi Moshe did not know their names. So many students now came here to learn.

Most of the Jews now living in Fostat were not native to Egypt, but a few thousand of them had come in the last few years to learn with Rabbi Moshe.

Rabbi Moshe entered the large gray building that had been converted into a hostel under his initiative.

Here were Jews from all over the Islamic world, in tarbooshes and turbans. The men stood at attention as Rabbi Moshe walked among them.

A small round man with olive skin and thin lips hurried forward to Rabbi Moshe. He was a native of Damietta who had moved here to learn.

"Mar Akiva," said Rabbi Moshe, "I have come to look at the books."

"At once! They are in my office."

Mar Akiva led Rabbi Moshe through the dining room, where tens of students sat on carpets before platters of food.

As Rabbi Moshe passed through the hall, they hurried to their feet.

Rabbi Moshe stopped and asked a teenaged student with lambent eyes, "Is the food adequate?"

"Yes, yes, very good," the student stumbled over his words.

In the office, Mar Akiva opened a ledger, and Rabbi Moshe

bent over it. "This is the record for food expenses," Rabbi Moshe said. "What about the accounts of the clothing that we provide to the students?"

Mar Akiva brought out another ledger and opened it.

Rabbi Moshe studied the figures and looked up at Mar Akiva. "Overall, how much are your expenses per year?"

"About ten thousand Egyptian dinars."

Rabbi Moshe nodded and closed the ledgers. He took out a stack of coins and put it on the table. "Give me a receipt for this money. It will go to any particularly poor Jew."

Out in the street again, Rabbi Moshe passed through the marketplace. A horde of Moslem beggars surrounded him. "Rabbi Moshe! The Jewish holy man is here! Help us, Rabbi Moshe!"

Rabbi Moshe reached into his robe and distributed coins among them.

"May the Compassionate G-d bless you with all good!" an old man pronounced, his face pock-marked. The others chorused, "Amen, may it be the Compassionate One's will!"

At the entrance to the city, amidst the tens of merchants mounting and alighting from donkeys, a snake charmer in a ragged turban opened his eyes wide as a thick snake sluggishly crawled up his forearm and onto his neck.

Here too a group of dusty beggars, Jewish and Moslem, gathered about Rabbi Moshe—"the Jewish holy man"—and he distributed coins among them.

Every week, Rabbi Moshe gave the poor Jews and Moslems a total of two hundred small Fez dinars.

Now Rabbi Moshe turned back to Fostat. After a short walk, he came to a building whose lintel was still charred from the firebombing that had taken place almost a decade before.

Here, swaying back and forth, a group of students was rehearsing a *sugya* from the *Gemara*. Seated on carpets were a rabbi and a group of students, learning the *halachos* of property rights. They sprang to their feet. Rabbi Moshe motioned with his hand. "Please keep learning." He walked through the halls of the *beis midrash,* listening to the students learn.

Then he was on the street again, passing by small boys who carried jars of water. From the leather market came the pungent smell of newly-cured hides, and Rabbi Moshe passed among small shops before which were set out belts, leather bags, straps and saddles.

Rabbi Moshe entered another *beis midrash* that he had established, and he circulated among the students.

Rabbi Moshe visited all the *batei midrash* that he had opened: five altogether. Here were not only young students but older men who had for a period of time set aside their craft to learn under Rabbi Moshe.

In two of the *batei midrash,* Rabbi Moshe sat down and delivered a *shiur* on the Rif to the students.

Before a group of thirty students, a rabbi told Rabbi Moshe, "We have received the following question. A man divorced his wife. Then, after she remarried and had children, he grew jealous of her. He has issued a document signed by two reputable witnesses that the signatories to the divorce are people who publicly transgress the Torah.

"He demands that the woman be forced to separate from her new husband and that her new children be declared illegitimate. How do you rule?"

Rabbi Moshe remained silent a moment and then answered, "It was a great mistake to have allowed sinful men to sign the divorce papers, for the testimony of such men cannot be accepted.

"If these men sinned without being warned, or if they merely have an evil reputation, the divorce is valid. The first husband is merely obligated to write his wife a new bill of divorce with kosher witnesses. She can remain married to her new husband and her children are not *mamzerim.*

"If, however, the two sinful witnesses were warned ahead of time that what they were about to do was punishable by lashes or excision, and they sinned anyway, then they are not kosher witnesses. In such an unlikely case, the divorce did not take place. The woman must leave her second husband, and the children are *mamzerim.*" (*Teshuvos Harambam* 3)

By positing extremely unlikely circumstances in which the witnesses would be declared unkosher, Rabbi Moshe was able to save a woman and her new family from being the victims of a vindictive former husband.

"Come out and see," one of his students wrote, "the beauty of the prince of princes . . . he is inheritor of the crown, Moshe—our rabbi, our commentator, our guide. He is the beauty of the age and its wonder. His name has risen to the heavens. He is the candle of the west and the light of the east. He rejoices like the man of might to run upon the path. He is the crown of the wise men and the prince who commands the nations." (letter of Rabbi Antoli in *Igros Uteshuvos Harambam*)

15

The Mishneh Torah

THE YEAR WAS 1180.

A brass lamp hung from the ceiling, its yellow flame burning still and motionless.

Three scribes were bent over their parchments, copying from a manuscript. One of them finished a sheet and set it aside. The other scribes glanced at where he had gotten up to and hurried their writing.

In another room of the *beis midrash,* Rabbi Moshe reviewed the introduction to his work. Ten years he had labored on this work—ten years of financial hardship, private tragedy, political revolution and leadership of the Jews of Cairo.

In an age when Jews were unlearned and unsure about how to keep the commandments, Rabbi Moshe had composed a work that explained the *halachos* clearly, in an arrangement that made any topic simple to look up.

At the beginning of this undertaking, he had set out his goals in the Introduction to *Sefer Hamitzvos.*

"After composing the *Pirush Hamishnayos*," he had written, "I have decided to compile all the laws of the Torah. I shall attempt, as is my custom, not to mention disagreements or discarded opinions, but only to set down the decided *halachah*. In this way, this compilation will include all the laws of the Torah of Moshe Rabbeinu.

"I have decided not to compose this work in the Holy Tongue [of *Tanach*], since that sanctified language is too narrow for us today to explicate all the details of the laws. Nor will I compose it in the language of the Talmud [Aramaic], since only a few individuals today understand it, and many words are unusual even for those familiar with the Talmud. But I shall compose it in the language of the *Mishneh*, so that it will be easy for most people.

"I will include all that is established and clarified from the words of the Torah, so that no question will be missing.

"It is my purpose to combine abridgment with completeness, so that the reader will encompass all that is found in the *Mishneh*, the Talmud, the *Sifra*, the *Sifrei* and the *Tosefta*, as well as all that the later *Geonim* added.

"In short, there should be no need after the Torah for any other *sefer* besides this one to learn whatever *halachos* one needs to know, whether of Torah or of rabbinic origin."

Rabbi Moshe decided to arrange the work topically. He explained, "I considered how this work should be arranged: whether I should divide it according to the division of the *Mishneh* or according to topic. It became clear to me that it will be best to divide it under the headings of different *halachos.*"

Copies were sent out all over the world. In Spain, Yehudah Alcharizi, author of *Tachkemoni*, sang of the great impression that the work had made:

THE RAMBAM

*He sifted the entire Talmud like flour through a sieve
And took from it clear, fine flour,
Preparing a ready-made meal for those who deal with halachic
   questions.
The children of Israel ate the manna
Which they hadn't toiled over, and they did not err.
He left out the names of the commentators
As well as discussions and arguments
That confuse a person's thought,
And presented the gist of the Talmud clearly.*

Letters poured in from the land of Israel, Arabia, Spain and France, thanking Rabbi Moshe for the work that he had done.

Three messengers from Yemen rested in an inn south of Giza. They had been sent with a special message of thanks from the Yemenite community to Rabbi Moshe for his *Mishneh Torah,* and with instructions to buy a number of copies of the fourteen-volume work.

Rabbi Moshe meanwhile reread the sheet that he held in his hand. A scholar had once asked him in irritation, "I don't understand what you are spending your time on. We already have the written Torah, the *Mishneh,* the Talmud and the writings of the Geonim. When a Jew has a question in *halachah,* he has to look for the answer. Then he studies the *halachah* and all the questions and arguments about different points of the *halachah,* until he comes to a conclusion. But you are setting down the *halachos* like a guidebook, one after the other, without even bringing the source!"

Rabbi Moshe's answer to that rabbi was contained in the Introduction which he now was reviewing.

"In this time, there have been many sorrows," Rabbi Moshe had written. "Everyone has been adversely affected. As a result, the wisdom of the Sages and the understanding of the men of discernment have been lost.

"Those commentaries and *halachos* and responsa that the

Geonim considered to be easily understandable are today understood correctly only by a small number of people.

"How much more is this the case regarding the Talmud itself: the Babylonian and Jerusalem Talmuds, the *Sifra*, the *Sifrei*, and the *Tosefta*.

"One needs broad knowledge, a wise spirit and a great deal of time in order to be able to arrive at the correct understanding regarding what is forbidden or allowed and the other laws of the Torah.

"I have called this work, *Mishneh Torah*—the Review of the Torah," Rabbi Moshe concluded, "for a person may read the written Torah first and then this, and he will know the entire Oral Torah. He needs to read no other work than these."

A thousand miles eastward, on the Malabar coast of Southwest India, two merchants wearing Indian robes of fine red silk sat together on a patio, studying the *Mishneh Torah*.

In Aden, a group of Jews chanted the words of the *Mishneh Torah*. The greatest *talmid chacham* among them, who worked as a silversmith, had punctuated the vowels with the ancient Babylonian system of vowels above—and not below—the letters. They pronounced the words with the pronunciation of the soft *daled*, the sibilant *tzadi* and guttural *gimmel* that had been forgotten over the years in other communities.

In Posquierres, France, the major scholars studied the *Mishneh Torah*, wondering that Rabbi Moshe should have left out all his sources.

In Baghdad, a scholar in an oval rabbinic cap rose from his seat and exclaimed in agitation, "Who is this Rabbi Moshe who speaks with such great authority without consulting my teacher, Rabbi Shmuel ben Eli?"

A student in Kairouan complained to his friend, "I do not understand. If the *Mishneh Torah* is meant to teach practical *halachah*, then why are so many sections devoted to the *halachos* that are not in force right now: the *halachos* of the Beis Hamikdash, sacrifices, the laws of ritual purity and the laws relating to the Sanhedrin?"

The other student smiled back. "Have you not seen Rabbi Moshe's *Igeres Teiman*? He writes there that the time of the Mashiach will soon be coming. Don't you worry. These parts of the *Mishneh Torah* will be practicable sooner than you expect!"

Rabbi Moshe composed the *Mishneh Torah* not only as a *halachic* guide but as a guide to life. In his opening chapters, he included an overview of the Jewish view of G-d and the world. He outlined the grandeur of the physical universe, utilizing the view most accepted in his day, the Aristotelian model. He described the astronomical universe and the qualities of the four basic elements.

He wrote of the necessity to lead a moral and balanced life, the famous "middle path": "A man might think that since jealousy, lust, honor and the like are evil and take a man out of the world, he should remove himself from them entirely, until he will not eat meat, drink wine, marry, live in a pleasant dwelling, wear good clothing and the like, as do pagan priests. But this too is an evil path." (*Hilchos Deios* 3:1)

One should strive to be healthy—not merely for one's convenience, but in order to be able to serve G-d well. One should have a son—not with the intent that the son will help support the household, but rather that he may become a great *talmid chacham.*

As for physical health, it is "a vital part of serving G-d," Rabbi Moshe wrote, for "it is impossible to understand and gaze at the teachings of wisdom when one is hungry or ill or if any of one's limbs ache."

When a person devotes his entire life to G-d, Rabbi Moshe wrote, "he is serving G-d constantly—even when he is engaged in business or family matters. His constant intent is that when he takes care of his needs, his body will be healthy and able to serve G-d. If he sleeps with the intent that he will not get sick but will be able to serve G-d, his sleep is itself a service of G-d. Our Sages said of this idea, 'All your acts should be for the sake of heaven.' (*Avos* 2:12) Shlomo Hamelech said, 'In all your ways, know Him, and He shall make your path straight.' (*Mishlei* 3:6)

Rabbi Moshe did not neglect any area of life that could affect one's well-being.

From Aydhab, a trader in brazilwood wrote to his wife in Alexandria, "Take heed of the following words of the *Mishneh Torah*, and may G-d keep you and the family in good health.

"'Only eat when you are hungry and drink when you are thirsty. Do not eat to the point that your belly is full, but leave a fourth unsatisfied. Do not eat until you have taken a walk or done some work in order to warm your body.'"

The merchant wrote, "Be sure to practice food combining according to the words of Rabbi Moshe: 'Foods such as melons should be eaten a little while before the meal, and not together with the meal. In the summer, one should eat cold foods and in the rainy season, one should eat hot foods and many spices.'"

The spirit of the service of G-d permeates the entirety of the *Mishneh Torah*, culminating in the words at the end of the work, describing the days of the Mashiach:

"The Sages and prophets desired the days of the Mashiach not in order to eat, drink and rule over the world, but in order to be free to learn Torah and its wisdom without the troubles of famine or war, with no jealousy and fighting; but rather with goodness freely flowing, with learned people as common as the dust. Then the Jews will only learn Torah. There will be great Sages whose understanding of the intent of their Creator will reach the height that human intellect can attain, as in the verse, 'The earth will be filled with knowledge of G-d like water covering the sea.'"

Never had such an all-inclusive work of *halachah* been written. From the labyrinth of Talmudic and post-Talmudic literature, Rabbi Moshe drew a map that was a clear description of Jewish law.

A Spanish student of the *Mishneh Torah* wrote ecstatically, "Before this work came to Spain, the learning of the Talmud was so hard for the Jews here that they had to rely only on what the rabbis said, for they did not know how to find clear *halachah* from the complex discussions. But when they learned the composition of the Rambam, which was understandable to them in a simple language, and were amazed at its beautiful order, their eyes were opened, and they recognized its great worth. They studied it deeply; youth and elders gathered to learn it. Now there increased people who know Torah, who can themselves make *halachic* decisions and study the *halachic* decisions of the judges. And just as in Spain, so was this everywhere, even in the Eastern lands, where they spend more time learning Talmud. The praise of the great teacher grew day by day, in particular when it became gradually known that his private life is in keeping with the ideal of a scholar as he describes in his work." (*Harambam Vedoro*)

Letters poured in to Rabbi Moshe, praising him as "unique in the generation," "the ensign of the rabbis," and "the enlightener of the eyes of the Jews."

Rabbi Aharon ben Meshullam of Lunel wrote, "From the day that the Talmud was sealed, there was not composed such an exalted composition as the Rambam's *Mishneh Torah*."

But there were also those who attacked the *Mishneh Torah*.

One of the most respected critics was the Raavad, Rabbi Avraham ben David of Posquierre, one of the leading *talmidei chachamim* of France, a wealthy and powerful Torah leader.

"The Rambam intended to fix, but he did not fix," the Raavad wrote. "He brought sources without citing them. He chose between opinions—but why should we assume his choice to be correct?"

The sharp notes that the Raavad wrote are today known as *Hasagos Haraavad* and are printed alongside the *Mishneh Torah*.

But despite the pointed tone of many of his statements, the Raavad admitted, "he has done a great work in gathering the words of the *Gemara*, the *Yerushalmi* and the *Tosefta*."

Rabbi Moshe was sensitive to the criticism he received. "I will not boast that I have never erred," Rabbi Moshe wrote later in a letter to his student Rabbi Yosef. "To the contrary, if it is made clear to me that I was mistaken, I will admit my error, whether it be an error in my work, in my personality or even in my nature." (*Igros Uteshuvos*)

He wrote later as well, "For ten straight years, I worked day and night to put this work together. But who can be free of errors? One forgets, particularly when one grows older. For all these reasons, it is fitting to examine my words and to check after me. The scholars have done me a great favor [with their critical comments]. I will be grateful to whoever finds anything and lets me know about it, so that there will be no stumbling block, G-d forbid, for my only purpose in this work was to open the roads." (*Teshuvah* 48)

But Rabbi Moshe had no patience for those who exploited the Torah to show off their own knowledge.

One day, Rabbi Moshe sat in the *beis midrash*. On the indigo wall behind him, verses from *Tanach* were painted in intricate letters painted of gold. About him sat a dozen laymen: merchants, craftsmen and donkey drivers.

Toward Rabbi Moshe's right sat a man with sharp eyes. Rabbi Moshe read from his *Mishneh Torah* and commented briefly. As he spoke, this man looked around at the others with a narrow smile, nodding his head.

This man had come to Fostat from Cairo, where he enjoyed a reputation as a Talmud scholar. Here too, it seemed, he must claim for himself the attention of all those about him. One moment, he nodded his head sagely; the next, he shook his head in annoyance, as though he had come to pass judgment on Rabbi Moshe.

Rabbi Moshe came to a new paragraph. He read the *halachah* and briefly explained what it meant.

This was the visiting scholar's chance. Clearing his throat, he leaned forward and shook a finger until he caught Rabbi Moshe's attention.

"If I may be so bold," he stretched out his vowels, "there are a number of Talmudic passages that form the basis of this *halachah*, as is known to those well-versed in the *Gemara*. Would you be so kind as to enter into a discussion of those passages?"

Rabbi Moshe looked back into the man's eyes. "If it had been my intent to surround the *Mishneh Torah* with commentary from the Talmud, then what would have been the point of writing it in the first place?" (*Igros Harambam*, based on a letter written by Rabbi Avraham ben Harambam, p. 254)

The *Mishneh Torah* was intended not as a complex Talmudic work, but as a simple and definitive *halachic* guide.

But with the passage of time came written attacks and defenses of the work. Today the *Mishneh Torah* is surrounded by a collection of commentaries. More than that, the *Mishneh Torah* is not the sole *halachic* sourcebook, having been succeeded by the *Arba Turim* and, following that, the *Shulchan Aruch*.

But the *Mishneh Torah* is still one of the primary texts of *halachah*, and a model of clarity and form.

Many *talmidei chachamim,* particularly of the school of Brisk, have made a specialty of analyzing the careful language—the "golden tongue"—of the *Mishneh Torah.* They infer *halachos* and interpretations from the way the *Mishneh Torah* makes a statement and under what rubric a statement is made—or from analyzing what statement has been omitted.

The clarity and authority of the *Mishneh Torah* were a function of Rabbi Moshe's love for his fellow Jews. He made sure to communicate in a way that would be easily understandable.

To this day, his *Mishneh Torah* is a masterwork and a basic *halachic* text that is universally revered.

16

A Letter of Support

AT ABOUT THIS TIME, RABBI MOSHE AND A DELEGATION OF RABBIS
petitioned the government to remove the corrupt Zuta from
the post of *nagid.*

Saladin was no longer in Cairo. In 1177, he had led an army
out of Egypt to battle the Christians in the Holy Land and then
returned to his native Damascus.

Rabbi Moshe and his fellow rabbis presented their peti-
tion to the acting ruler of Egypt, Vizier Alfadil, in his reception
chamber.

Alfadil stroked his long jaw. "I shall consider the matter."

The next day, he summoned Zuta before him.

"Zuta," Alfadil said, leaning back on an elbow, "the Chief
Rabbi of Fostat claims that you are oppressing the Jews. He
says that you have no mandate from them and that they do not
desire you to continue serving as *nagid.* I have considered the

matter. You are dismissed from the post."

Zuta exchanged a desperate glance with his son. "But your excellence!" he exclaimed. "Do not forget the small contribution that your humble servant has made every year to your royal coffers . . ."

Zuta was referring to the bribe of two hundred dinars that he paid annually to keep the post of *nagid.*

But Alfadil's attention had turned, and he was conferring with one of his aides. Perhaps Alfadil hadn't heard him? But it would never do to raise his voice. That might cost his head.

Defeated, Zuta backed away from before the vizier, his face gray and sweaty.

A few days later, Zuta returned to the vizier.

"Your excellence," Zuta said, "I am most distressed that I must give you news that will—I am sorry to report—reflect badly on my fellow-religionists."

"What is it?" Alfadil asked in an unfriendly voice.

"There are traitors who skulk throughout your kingdom, remnants of the discarded Shiite caliph, may his bones be ground to dust.

"Your excellence, my loyalty to your great rulership forces me to utter the words that I wish I did not have to say."

"Well?" barked Alfadil.

Zuta bowed his eyes to the ground. "The Jews of Fostat and Cairo are harboring these enemies of the kingdom. The Jews secretly feed them and provide them shelter. Not one of the Jews will tell you. But I have come forward today to reveal this conspiracy."

Alfadil leaned forward. "Why have I not heard of this before?"

"Because the Jews are so clannish, your excellence. But I am not part of their cabal. That is the true reason that they approached you some days ago and incited you to remove me from my post. They know that if I am not *nagid,* no one will be able to oppose their schemes."

For long minutes, Alfadil swayed back and forth, stroking his long chin.

"Very well," he pronounced at last. "You may return to your post."

At about this time, Rabbi Moshe received a letter from a man who lived in Jerusalem named Rabbi Ovadiah.

"I am a convert from Islam," he wrote to Rabbi Moshe. "Since I was born to Moslem parents, in the prayers how can I recite the phrases in the prayerbook, 'Our G-d and the G-d of our fathers,' 'Who sanctified us with His commandments,' and 'Who brought us out of the land of Egypt'?

"And I have another question as well that my own rabbi has not answered satisfactorily."

Ovadiah had approached his rabbi after the morning *shiur,* which had dealt with the laws of idol worship.

"Rabbi Eliezer," Ovadiah said. "Would you consider Moslems to be idol worshippers?"

"Certainly they are," Rabbi Eliezer replied quickly and made a movement as if to leave the *beis midrash.*

Ovadiah raised a hand, as if to stop him. "I don't understand how that could be. I was raised as a Moslem, and I know what they believe. They believe in only one G-d."

"Don't bother me with nonsense, Ovadiah," Rabbi Eliezer replied. "Obviously, they are idol worshippers when their whole religion is riddled with idolatry."

"But, Rabbi," Ovadiah persisted, and laid his hand on Rabbi Eliezer's arm.

"Ach!" Rabbi Eliezer jerked his arm free of Ovadiah's hand. "You want to get into a discussion with me about this?" he said in an angry voice. "Then I suppose I'm willing. After all, the verse tells us, 'Answer a fool according to his folly.'" (*Mishlei* 26:5)

Ovadiah turned away from Rabbi Eliezer, deeply shamed.

169

"There's no need," he forced himself to say in a dead voice.

Days later, he was still dejected. It was then that he poured out his heart in a letter to Rabbi Moshe, the great and compassionate leader that he had heard so much about.

Rabbi Moshe wrote, "I have received the questions of Rabbi Ovadiah, the wise and understanding righteous convert, may his recompense be complete from G-d, the Lord of Israel, under Whose Wings he has come to take refuge.

"You should pray like any other Jew without changing a word. Avraham Avinu taught and enlightened the entire world. He told them the true path and the Oneness of the Holy Blessed One. He rejected idolatry and brought many under the Wings of G-d's Presence.

"Therefore, whoever converts to the end of generations and whoever unifies G-d's Name, as is written in the Torah, is the student of Avraham Avinu and a member of his household.

"You should say, 'Our G-d and the G-d of our fathers,' for Avraham is your father.

"As for 'Who took us out of Egypt,' if you wish, you may say, 'Who took Israel out of Egypt.' But if you do not change it, you lose nothing thereby. Since you have entered under the Wings of G-d's Presence and are following G-d, there is no difference between us and you. All the miracles were as though both for us and for you.

"Most of our forefathers who left Egypt were idol-worshippers. They mixed with non-Jews and learned from them until G-d sent Moshe Rabbeinu, who separated us from the nations and placed us under the Wings of G-d's Presence—us and all converts, and made us all as one.

"Do not let your lineage be unimportant in your eyes. If we are related to Avraham, Yitzchak and Yaakov, you are connected to the One Who spoke and created the universe. As is written in Yeshayahu (44:5), 'This one will say, I am Hashem's, and that one will be called by the name of Yaakov.' The convert will say, 'I am Hashem's,' and the born Jew will be called by the name of Yaakov.

"As for your second question, the Moslems are not idol worshippers at all. This has already been removed from their mouths and hearts, and they declare that G-d is One, as is proper. Although they lie about us, claiming that we believe that G-d has a son, this is no reason for us to lie about them and say that they are idol worshippers.

"Your rabbi answered you disrespectfully and made you sorrowful, calling you a fool.

"This is a great sin. He should ask your forgiveness, even though you are his student. Then he should fast, cry out and pray. Perhaps G-d will forgive him.

"Was he drunk that he did not know of the thirty-six places that the Torah speaks of the convert? And what is the word of G-d: 'Do not oppress the convert' (*Shemos* 22:20), which refers to oppressive speech?

"Even if he spoke the truth and you were in error, he should have spoken kindly and softly. How much more when you spoke the truth and he erred!

"Before he investigated whether the Moslems are idol worshippers, he should have investigated his own anger that led him to unjustly insult a righteous convert. Our Sages have said, 'Whoever becomes angry should be considered as an idol worshipper.' (*Shabbos* 105b)

"We are commanded to honor and fear our father and mother, and to listen to the prophets. It is possible that a person will honor, fear and listen to someone whom he doesn't love. But we are commanded to love the convert: 'You shall love the convert' (*Devarim* 10:19), just as we are commanded to love G-d: 'You shall love G-d your Lord.'

"G-d loves the convert, as written in the verse, 'He loves the convert, to give him bread and clothing.' (*Devarim* 10:18)

"As for the fact that your rabbi called you a fool: this is astonishing.

"You left your father, your birthplace and your powerful nation, and understood with the eye of your heart. You came and cleaved to this nation, which is today 'a despised people . . . a slave of rulers.' (*Yeshayahu* 49:7) You knew that its religion is the true and righteous religion. You ran after G-d, passed on the holy path and entered under the Wings of G-d's Presence, rolled in the dust of the feet of Moshe Rabbeinu and desired His commandments. Your soul impelled you to approach G-d, to be enlightened by the light of life, to rise to the level of the angels and to rejoice with the joy of the righteous.

"You flung this world away from your heart and did not turn to the empty vanities and false passions.

"And will such a person be called a fool?

"Heaven forbid! Not 'fool' has G-d called your name, but wise, understanding and intelligent, walking straight, the student of Avraham Avinu, who himself abandoned his forefathers and birthplace and turned after G-d."

One day, two years after Zuta had been returned to office, there was a commotion in the streets.

People ran forward to a knot of soldiers, leading between them three poor, disheveled Jews. Two of them walked silently with hopeless eyes. But the third Jew was yelling and hitting out at the soldiers. They circled him, and as one of the soldiers grabbed him from behind, another soldier hit him across the face. Only then did the man fall silent, blood streaming from his nose. Half-held up by the guard from behind, he stumbled forward, and the soldiers continued leading the prisoners.

A terrified Jew ran to the home of Rabbi Yitzchak ben Rabbi Sasson Hadayan. Rabbi Yitzchak rushed out of the house to save the Jews. But by the time he came to the gates of Cairo, the prisoners were no longer in sight.

"Where are the prisoners who were taken from our community?" he demanded at the gate of the palace.

A high-ranking soldier finally came out to Rabbi Yitzchak. "They are being held in the dungeon until their case shall be dealt with."

The dungeon! Who did not speak of the dungeon without fear—an infested pit where one's soul was tormented and one's body broken, where one talked willingly or unwillingly, where one cried out all confessions and groveled without shame?

"Of what crime are they accused?" Rabbi Yitzchak asked.

"Treason."

In the palace, Zuta and his son stood before Vizier Alfadil. "Your royal highness," Zuta bowed his head, his oily pate gleaming darkly, "we delight in bringing you news that will please you.

"Due to the concerted efforts of myself and my honorable son, we have captured three spies from foreign lands whom the Jews have been harboring. Even as I speak, they lie in chains in your dungeon, ready to confess their crimes and indict their Jewish co-conspirators."

"You have done me a great service, Zuta."

Zuta bowed his head further and stepped backward, his son beside him. His brown, bald head receded like a disappearing spot of grease in the white brilliance of the royal chamber.

Two days later, having been starved and beaten, the three prisoners died. The Jewish community was terrified. But with great courage, Rabbi Yitzchak led the campaign against Zuta and his son.

He and the other leaders of Fostat, including Rabbi Moshe, met in the synagogue. Holding *Sifrei Torah*, they excommunicated the corrupt Zuta and his despicable son.

Zuta responded by having two Jews killed on the pretext that they had concealed spies.

Rabbi Yitzchak gathered all the Jews of Fostat in the central synagogue, and they fasted and cried out to G-d.

At last, the Jews' prayers and efforts were answered, and Zuta was removed from his post.

(This information is contained in a letter published in *Chadashim Gam Yashanim*, by Rabbi A. Harkavy. Since the letter is fragmentary, exactly what occurred or why it was Rabbi Yitzchak and not Rabbi Moshe who took a leading role in this case is not known.)

17

Philosophy

SUNLIGHT SPARKLED AGAINST THE BURNISHED CHANDELIER. RABBI
Moshe sat on a sky-blue mat from the center of which radiated
a sixteen-pointed star in vivid crimson and olive-green.

"Lesson ended!" Rabbi Moshe slapped his hand down on
the rug and stood up, adjusting his khaki robe.

"Rabbi Moshe, may I speak with you?" It was a young man
with a soft, short beard.

"Yes, Yosef, what is it?" Rabbi Moshe came up to Rabbi
Yosef's side, squeezing his arm affectionately, and they walked
together sedately from the *beis midrash*.

Rabbi Yosef ben Rabbi Yehudah ibn Shimon was one of
Rabbi Moshe's outstanding students. (He is often confused
with Rabbi Yosef ibn Aknin. However, these were two
different men. Rabbi Yosef ibn Aknin was the same age as
Rabbi Moshe and had befriended him in Fez.)

Rabbi Yosef had travelled from the city of Sabta, in Morocco, to learn under Rabbi Moshe. Arriving in Alexandria, he wrote impassioned poetry to Rabbi Moshe, telling of his great desire to learn Torah.

"When I first received your letters," Rabbi Moshe subsequently told Rabbi Yosef, "I was very impressed by them, yet I still feared that your desire for learning may be greater than your capability."

When Rabbi Yosef at last arrived in Fostat, he reviewed before Rabbi Moshe his knowledge of Torah, astronomy and mathematics.

"Then," Rabbi Moshe recalled, "I was filled with joy at your quick intelligence. I saw your intense desire to learn the secular sciences, and I allowed you to do so.

"When you demonstrated to me what you had learned of the science of logic, I saw that I shall be able to teach you the secrets of the works of prophecy. I began to teach you with certain hints, and I still saw you desiring more knowledge. You begged me to teach you these Divine matters.

"Then I saw you entering into areas of confusion. I made sure to explain everything in the Torah in a clear, direct manner that would reveal the truth of the Torah." (paraphrased from a letter by Rambam to Rabbi Yosef, *Igros Harambam, Shailat*, p. 220)

Rabbi Yosef stood before Rabbi Moshe with a look of consternation.

"Rabbi Moshe, I am afraid that I shall have to leave you."

"What do you mean?"

"I have to travel to Aleppo."

They entered the street. A palace official in a crimson robe hurried up to Rabbi Moshe. "Are you the Chief Rabbi?" he demanded.

"Yes. What is it?"

"The vizier is ill, and none of his physicians have satisfied him. A royal carriage is waiting at the gates of Fostat to take you to him immediately."

Rabbi Moshe turned to Rabbi Yosef. "We shall speak again." He hurried after the court official.

In his chamber, Alfadil lay in bed, surrounded by three physicians. He turned his head to the door. "Rabbi Moshe, are you here? Your brother-in-law, Abu Almaali, has informed me that you are an excellent physician."

"I practice to the best of my ability."

"Step forward and examine me."

Rabbi Moshe carefully questioned Alfadil about his symptoms and his daily regimen. How much did he sleep? How many meals a day did he eat, and exactly what did he eat? Did he do any exercise, and if so, what kind? Then he examined Alfadil, taking his pulse and checking the color of his tongue.

"What is it?" Alfadil asked in a worried voice. "Am I very ill?"

"Your majesty is basically of a sound constitution," Rabbi Moshe replied, "but you must rearrange your daily schedule. I shall advise certain changes in your diet and shall also write remedies for some of your specific conditions."

"What do you mean?"

"For instance, for your problems in digestion and asthma, I shall prescribe a remedy recommended by Galen, prepared from the inner parts of dried figs, wild-growing olives, raisins and the small fruit of dogwood."

"And this will heal me?" Alfadil asked.

"This will contribute significantly to your improvement," Rabbi Moshe replied. "But I shall also prescribe other changes in your life. For instance, you must breathe fresh air, neither too warm nor too cool. On a hot day such as today, the floor of your room should be sprayed and sprinkled with scented water and a draft allowed to blow through the room.

"But more important, you must take good care of your

psychological well-being. When a person suffers mentally, he loses his appetite for food. He is too upset to exercise correctly. He is bent over and he does not breathe correctly.

"But when your highness will be filled with gladness and liveliness, your heart will be quickened, your circulation stimulated and your mental acuity sharpened."

Alfadil sat up in his bed. "How do I attain such a state of mind?" he asked eagerly.

"Your highness must train yourself in the philosophical virtues: ethics, morals and the like. In this way, you will learn the nature of your psyche. The knowledge and maturity that you gain shall guard you from extreme emotional states, which are harmful to the health.

"When you gain this measure of stoicism, you will not take to heart the passing phenomena of this world. Such matters as 'good fortune' and 'bad fortune' will recede from your heart. In the world of the mind, they will become no more than evanescent phantoms." (based on the Rambam's *Treatise on Asthma*, edited by Suessman Muntner)

Three days later, Vizier Afadil again summoned Rabbi Moshe to his palace. The vizier sat upon his throne, his eye clear and his complexion ruddy.

"I am glad to see your highness looking so well."

"I am more than satisfied with your advice," Alfadil said. "I hereby appoint you to the council of physicians who treat me and the royal family."

When Rabbi Moshe returned to Fostat, he was greeted with joy by the Jews. What an honor—that their rabbi should be one of the physicians of the vizier!

Yet Rabbi Moshe did not rejoice. One evening, one of the leading citizens of Fostat approached him. "Rabbi Moshe, don't you share our pride in your attainment?"

"It is not so simple," Rabbi Moshe said. "When Jews are gaining high positions in these times, I do not consider that a success. It is a rather great drudgery and toil."

"But to be physician to the vizier!" the man protested. "If that isn't success, what is?"

"What is success?" Rabbi Moshe mused. "Success is that of the spiritual life: to be a good Jew and to do what one is obligated to do. One reaches success when one is far from the crowd, far from degraded paths and unpleasant personalities. A man who is in a position of leadership only increases his troubles. He is always in danger of being insulted by non-Jews and falling into the hands of the government, which is liable to jail him—even to torture him!"

"But still," the man chuckled nervously, "when a person is liked."

"Even then," Rabbi Moshe said. "For when one acts in order to please other people, one is already opposing the Torah of G-d. As G-d admonished Eli Hakohen, 'You have honored your sons more than you have honored Me.'" (*Shmuel I* 2:29) (from letter to Rabbi Yosef, p. 262)

Besides this, Rabbi Moshe's new post took up a great deal of his time—and because it was considered such a great honor, he received no pay. Yet neither could he decline the request of the vizier.

Rabbi Moshe's new attainment was bittersweet for another reason. It was mixed with the sadness of the departure of his beloved student Rabbi Yosef.

For the last time, the two men walked together through the Herbalists' Bazaar, where under a bronze sign reading "Spices, Herbs, Medical Plants," bags were filled with yellow, fist-sized chunks of brimstone and aquamarine pebbles of sulphate copper.

"My teacher," Rabbi Yosef said. "My greatest regret in leaving you is that I shall not again listen to your illuminating wisdom reconciling the teachings of the Torah and of Aristotle."

Rabbi Moshe replied, "Do not be confused by the apparent inconsistencies between your secular knowledge and the teachings of the Torah. The sciences are merely the handmaidens of the Torah."

"I believe you," Rabbi Yosef said. "Yet when I see that the teachings of Aristotle seem to support the Islamic faith and to contradict our Torah, how can I help but be confused?"

The sky was a strange, muted blue. In its peculiar glow, a damp breeze blew, and the rows of gray buildings seemed to be waiting impassively for the abrupt outburst of a storm.

Rabbi Moshe and Rabbi Yosef entered the textile bazaar, whose streets were entirely covered with sheets of tin, illuminated only by the uncertain flickering of oil lanterns and occasional skylights.

"You are right," Rabbi Moshe said. "You cannot leave in the midst of your studies."

"Yet I must!" Rabbi Yosef burst out.

"Do not be disconsolate. I shall write you a treatise dealing with your perplexities. As I complete each chapter, I shall mail it to you."

"I shall be most grateful."

The two men turned a corner and stepped out into the daylight. A baker was crying, "Fresh rolls!" On a tray before his shop lay two dozen pastries, still steaming, their flaky crusts crackling.

Swiftly, Rabbi Yosef turned to his teacher. "I shall miss you!"

The chapters that Rabbi Moshe sent his student eventually comprised his famous work of philosophy, *The Guide to the Perplexed.*

Rabbi Moshe also wrote to Rabbi Yosef regarding his monumental work of *halachah*, the *Mishneh Torah.* The main purpose of learning, he stated, was not to delight in clever arguments but to determine the meaning of the Talmud and the *halachah.*

"I have already told you," Rabbi Moshe wrote, "to keep learning this *sefer* until you know it entirely, and to teach it everywhere as well.

"The main purpose for which the Talmud and related *sefarim* were written down has been lost.

"Now the intent of those who learn is to waste their time in arguments—as though the purpose of learning the Talmud is to sharpen one's abilities to argue, and nothing else!

"But this is not the case. The give and take and the argument are incidental. Of course, when there are two views of a matter, the two sides need to argue in order to come to the truth of the matter. But now people think that the argument is the heart of Talmudic studies!" (letter to Rabbi Yosef, p. 257)

When Rabbi Moshe returned home one evening, a quarter moon was hanging high in a foggy sky, like a coin shining through a misty veil.

Entering the brightly-lit front room, he gazed in surprise at his visitor. "Rabbi Uziel! What an unexpected pleasure!"

Rabbi Uziel smiled. "Sometimes even the queen runs out of work to give me."

"And you brought your son."

Rabbi Uziel's son, a young man with a newly-growing beard, was already known as an outstanding medical student.

"Yes," Rabbi Uziel said. "G-d willing, he will be the personal physician of Chalij Arsalan in Alrov." (This son's Hebrew name is not known; his Arabic name was Abu Alrasa. He was Rabbi Moshe's nephew both through his sister and through his wife.)

Rabbi Moshe stayed up with his visitors until late into the evening. After they left, he shut the window shutter in the guestroom. In the sky, stars burned pale beyond the drifting mist.

In his own room, Rabbi Moshe and his wife, Jamilah, heard

their baby cough. "Is that the girl?" Rabbi Moshe asked.

"Yes," Jamilah said. "She's had a cough all day. But Avraham is sleeping soundly." Rabbi Moshe's baby boy, Avraham, had been born in *Sivan* of 1186.

"It doesn't sound bad," Rabbi Moshe said. "But I'll have a look at her tomorrow morning. Did you close the shutter in her room?"

"Of course."

A moist breeze snaked through their room. "Ugh!" Jamilah said. "I don't like it when the wind blows from the Nile. It's so damp and unhealthy." The copper lantern on the wall gave a shiver. She stepped to the window and gazed at the black shadows stretching across the courtyard, where there was in the daytime, she knew, the palm tree and the date tree. Now everything was velvety and mysterious. The child gave another cough. "The poor child!" Jamilah sighed.

The next morning, the girl's cough had gotten worse. Now Rabbi Moshe's infant son grew ill as well.

Nothing that Rabbi Moshe did sufficed to turn the decree from heaven. His infant daughter grew steadily sicker, until she passed away.

Avraham too grew deathly ill. For three days, Rabbi Moshe stayed at his bedside, night and day, tending to him. At last, the boy recovered from his illness.

Rabbi Moshe was worn out by the new tragedy he had endured. But he consoled himself, "G-d knows that every thinking person realizes that human life is good. There is more good than bad. Therefore a person has to understand the larger picture of the entire human species—and not just look at the fortunes of individuals." So did he write to his student, Rabbi Yosef. (*Igros Harambam*, p. 262) And he admonished him, "My son, do not mourn and do not be depressed regarding this matter."

Rabbi Moshe had other family problems to deal with. One

day, he received a letter from his sister, Miriam, who had not travelled with them to Egypt (it is not clear where she was living), with a letter about her son.

"To the wise man, the honored rabbi, Moshe, may G-d keep you, from she who is obligated to honor you, Miriam, your sister," she wrote.

"If you were to see me, you would not recognize me because of my terrible situation.

"The principal reason for this is my son, about whom I no longer hear anything, as though he is sunken into a pit. I have received no letter from him.

"I do not know where he is. This has caused me to weep and fast. He has gone from me, forgotten me and ceased to think of me, whether for good or evil.

"I only think that you may be able to help me in this matter, for you have the capability and you are a close relative.

"Please tell me what his situation is. Is he with you? Tell me, please. And if he has gone somewhere else, send him my letter and a letter of your own with words of rebuke that he should write me and tell me what he is doing.

"In your goodness, write to me. Make sure to find someone who will bring your letter to me, and tell me everything about your life. In this way, you will lighten my heart, silence my weeping and calm my pain and suffering. Do this, in your love and goodness.

"May you enjoy peace and strength.

"Send regards to Jamilah and to your brother, David, and to your sisters, may G-d keep them.

"And the person who is writing these lines, . . . ben Yaakov Chazan, sends regards to you all." (This letter, which was found in the *Cairo Genizah* by S.D. Goitein, appears in *Tarbitz*, 1963.)

18

Games of Chess

WHEN RABBI MOSHE WALKED INTO THE PALACE ONE MORNING, HE passed two courtiers in an antechamber bent over a chessboard.

On the board, two armies were engaged in combat. As the mysterious sultan (the king) hid in the last row, surrounded by rooks and elephants (knights), the all-powerful vizier (or queen) was free to range the board.

The Arabs played the game as a symbol of the battle between the two great empires: Christianity and Islam. But in India, where the game had originated, the chessboard represented the universe: the black and white squares represented day and night, and the two sides were the forces of good and evil engaged in cosmic battle.

One of the courtiers moved a pawn forward. "Checkmate!" he announced using the Persian-Arabic word. "*Ashakh mat*! The king is dead!"

The defeated player swept his king over, and the chess-man clattered onto the board.

The vizier had steadily grown to favor Rabbi Moshe over his other physicians. They murmured against Rabbi Moshe— "the Jew"—and he felt their hard stares and heard the rumors that friends brought him of their enmity. He could well imagine that they, too, longed to cry triumphantly, "Check-mate!"

In the royal chamber, Vizier Alfadil had not yet appeared. Beside his throne stood the cluster of physicians. When Rabbi Moshe entered the room, they turned as one to stare at him silently. Among them was an older man who was oddly familiar. Rabbi Moshe stepped forward with a half-smile on his lips.

"Abu Muisha!"

Yes, it was he—the Moslem who, twenty years earlier, had saved Rabbi Moshe's life in Morocco. How many hours had Rabbi Moshe spent together with him learning philosophy. And then, when he had been accused of being a secret Jew, Abu Muisha had stood up against the mob and defended him, at the risk of his own reputation.

The smile disappeared from Rabbi Moshe's face. Abu Muisha was staring back with a stony face. And why did he stand amidst the physicians?

But Moshe did not slacken his pace. "Abu Muisha! Can it be you? Do you not recognize me, Musa ben Maimon, whose life you saved in Fez?"

Abu Muisha's eyes were like black pebbles. "Yes, you are Musa ben Maimon, the lapsed Moslem."

The enormity of Abu Muisha's words staggered Rabbi Moshe. In the antechamber, the two courtiers had begun a new game of chess. Here a deadly game of chess was begin-ning, where the marble floor of the royal chamber constituted the chessboard, and the physicians and Abu Muisha were the pieces in black. They were already declaring "check"—we have surrounded the king.

Whom did Rabbi Moshe have on his side? Would the vizier be with him, or with them? That was the fateful question.

The vizier made his ceremonial entrance and seated himself on the throne.

The physicians bowed before him and introduced "the important philosopher from Morocco, Abu Muisha."

Abu Muisha stepped forward. "Your highness," he announced. "It is a great honor to stand here before you. I come to enlist your support in defense of the honor of Islam."

"Speak on," Alfadil said.

"Twenty years ago, a Moslem was accused in Fez of being a secret Jew. With great personal courage, I defended that Moslem and saved his life. Today that Moslem has become an openly-practicing Jew. Because of his high position, no one will whisper his name. But for the sake of the honor of Islam, I am willing to name him and demand that he suffer the penalty of that lapse from the faith."

"The penalty is death," mused Alfadil. "Whom do you accuse?"

Abu Muisha turned to face Rabbi Moshe with burning eyes and brusquely pointed his finger. "That is the man!"

Alfadil, always so measured and reserved, sat up straight in astonishment. "You accuse my royal physician and the chief rabbi of Fostat?"

"I am not concerned with what is politic, your highness. I am only concerned with what is right."

Alfadil regained his composure. "You have made an accusation, and the matter must be brought to a trial." Faint smiles appeared on the faces of several of the physicians. "Because Rabbi Moshe is such an important personage, the matter shall not go to the regular courts. Instead, he shall stand trial before my head judge, Magino, and I shall attend the proceedings."

Now the most important question had been answered. In this deadly game of living chess, the Vizier Aldafil would be on the side of Rabbi Moshe.

The matter swiftly came to trial.

Abu Muisha argued strenuously against Rabbi Moshe. "This man converted to Islam," he claimed (although that had not been the case). "If he has now lapsed, he must receive the supreme punishment."

But Judge Magino parried Abu Muisha's arguments. Finally, Vizier Alfadil, who was attending the trial, declared, "Rabbi Moshe maintains that he never converted to Islam, that being unknown in the city some people may have assumed he was Muslim, that he and his family never said one word that could be construed as a declaration of allegiance to Islam. I, for one, believe every world he has said. However, even if Rabbi Moshe had actually converted to Islam, he did so under extreme duress, and such a conversion would not be valid. Therefore, no punishment will fall on a person who retreats from such a forced action. The charges are dismissed."

To the north of Egypt, in the land of Israel, a different game of chess was being played: the decades-long war of the Crusades.

And now a battle took place that dramatically affected the Jews. Under Christian domination, the Jews had been largely barred from Jerusalem. But now, in a stunning reversal of fortune, Saladin crushed the Christian army.

It was a hot, dry day in July of 1187. In the midst of the Christian army rode the Bishop of Acco, bearing above his head the most sacred object in Christendom: a supposed relic of the cross on which the Nazarene had been crucified.

Opposing them, Saladin called upon the mercy of Allah in this *jihad*, this holy war.

THE RAMBAM

On the evening of the fourth of the month, the Christian army encamped on the hill of Hattin, five miles from the Galilee. Many of the men still wore their metal armor. Tens of thousands of soldiers lay in the stifling heat. The hill was bare and rocky, and the dust that they had kicked up irritated their throats.

Under the cover of the night, Saladin's troops surrounded the hill.

There was a burning red at the edge of the encampment. It swiftly blew up, spreading out, bursting all about the encampment. Fire! Saladin's troops were burning the dried, thick scrub at the foot of the hill. Great clouds of smoke were swept by the searing wind into the Christian camp.

The Christians rose to fight. But the heat of the flames suffocated them, and they struggled desperately to pull off their burning armor. And the thick smoke pouring over the hill choked them.

Within a few hours, half the Christian infantry surrendered, and the others soon followed.

Only the cavalry was left.

An Arab officer shouted, "Watch out! To your right!"

The Moslem soldiers turned. Bearing down on them were hundreds of Christian horsemen. In the fire and billowing smoke, they appeared to be fiendish apparitions.

Racing onto the Moslems, they swung their great swords, clearing a swathe littered with the suddenly killed and injured. There were howls of pain in the darkness.

The Moslems shot volleys of arrows at the horsemen, but the arrows either fell from their armor or pierced the armor without reaching the flesh.

When Saladin looked upon the scene, his initial victory seemed to be turning into a terrible rout. Later, his son, Malik Alafdal, recorded that Saladin "fell prey to despair. He changed color and clutched his beard as he advanced."

But now there was a wondrous sight: the Christian horsemen did not turn back to again attack the confused Moslems. It became suddenly clear that they were escaping. They were swallowed up into the dark night.

Saladin remained in control of the hill of Hattin, and his soldiers engaged the Christians in bloody, hand-to-hand combat, killing many and taking many others prisoner.

In the midst of battle, the terrible news was called out to the Christian soldiers: the relic of the cross had been captured by Saladin.

The Christians were seized with terror and despair. Some threw down their swords, others sank to their knees and cried out in a torment of betrayed faith, raising their arms to the heavens that were obscured by the clouds of smoke through which could be seen red, spinning sparks like the fires of damnation.

The dawn broke on a scene of indescribable carnage. The hill was littered with thousands of bloody corpses and disemboweled horses. Dead Christians and Moslems lay in the awkward positions of violent death. Others, with hideous injuries, moved among this charnel house like phantoms in a hellish tableau.

Wrote Saladin's son: "What a sweet scent of victory was exhaled by this charnel heap! What flames of vengeance flickered over these corpses! How men's hearts rejoiced at this hideous spectacle!"

Fifteen thousand Christians lay dead. Another fifteen thousand were prisoners. One Moslem stood guard over one or two hundred Christians. These noblemen who had condemned the Moslem faith—look at what they had come to now! "How many arrogant masters caught as though in a hunt, kings brought low and free men reduced to slavery, impostors delivered up to the true believers!" Saladin's son rejoiced.

Saladin in his tent was grim but satisfied. On this bloody day, he had at last broken the back of the Christian army. The army of the King of Jerusalem was scattered.

In Damascus, seat of power of Saladin and his army, the arrival of the spoils of war brought great happiness. "Every day," one Moslem wrote, "Christian heads were seen arriving, as numerous as watermelons. The spoils of oxen, sheep and goats and mules were so great that no one wanted any more." A statue of the Nazarene hanging on the cross was paraded about Damascus hung upside-down.

Now Saladin ruled the entire coast: Acco, Yaffa, Ashkelon and Beirut, as well as the Galilee and Shomron. Only Tyre was still controlled by the Christians.

Saladin turned his mind to the capture of the holiest city in Christendom—Jerusalem.

The Christians in Jerusalem numbered perhaps a hundred thousand—but they were mostly women and children. In addition, many of them were Greek Orthodox Christians who, having been for so many years oppressed by the Latin Christians, wished for a Moslem victory. There were at the most six thousand soldiers.

Outside the holy city, Saladin's troops were gathered, many thousands spread across the valley.

Saladin urged his troops to fight with vigor. Well did he have to urge them, for Jerusalem was merely the third-holiest city of Islam, and his troops were weary.

At last the siege began. The Moslems threw themselves against the city, but the Christians defended themselves wildly. "They fought like demons," a Moslem reported. "They prowled like wolves and acted like evil spirits. When their warriors drew their swords it was like the tumult of a raging sea. The priests urged them on, their leaders inflamed their spirits, their hearts rose to the fight. They set up an engine on every turret, dug deep trenches and raised pillars on all sides."

When the Moslems broke onto the narrow streets, their way was blocked by stones and trash.

But at last Jerusalem surrendered before Saladin. The entire population ransomed their lives with payment of ten dinars per man, five per woman and one per child.

In the ensuing bedlam, the Christian leaders who had offered to pay for the twenty thousand people who had no money evaded their promise. Most of these twenty-thousand people were sold into slavery.

Saladin now acted generously and nobly. He provided tens of thousands of Christians with charity, and with protection to help them return to Europe.

When the news reached the Jews of Fostat, Rabbi Moshe came before the vizier. "During the Christians' long occupation of the land," he said, "they did not allow the Jews to dwell in the holy city of Jerusalem. We now request that Islam, which is a just and righteous faith, allow the Jews who had been persecuted by the Christians to return to their ancient home."

The vizier sent messengers relaying the request of the Jews to the triumphant Sultan.

In his *Tachkemoni* (Gate 49), the poet Alcharizi wrote, "G-d awakened the spirit of the Sultan in the year 4950 [more exactly, 4947], and a spirit of inspiration and strength rested upon him. His army stormed Jerusalem, and G-d placed it in his hand.

"He then commanded that the following announcement should be made throughout the land to all, young and old: 'Speak to the heart of Jerusalem. Come to it, whoever desires, of the seed of Ephraim, those who remain from Ashur and Egypt, and the remnants from the ends of the heavens.'"

In *Tishrei* and *Marcheshvan* of 1188, Jews began straggling back to the ancient capital of the kingdom of Israel, and again they rebuilt the ruins of synagogues and study halls.

Elsewhere, another game of chess was taking place: a controversy in the world of Torah.

The white sun beat down on the white-washed houses topped with cupped roofs. Everywhere the sun glared, and men and women glided through the streets in white and black robes, their faces covered against the blinding light.

All the windows of the great *yeshivah* of Baghdad, the famous Gaon Yaakov, were opened, yet the air was motionless in the high-ceilinged hall. Shadows cast by marble colonnades lay in wide bands across the almost two thousand students who sat in even rows facing the *rosh yeshivah*, Rabbi Shmuel ben Eli.

Rabbi Shmuel ben Eli was clothed in golden and colored garments, like a king. He sat upon a gold-embroidered throne.

Next to him stood a tall interpreter. Rabbi Shmuel ben Eli spoke in a still voice to the interpreter, and this man repeated his words loudly for the students to hear.

One student whispered to his neighbor, "What did the *rosh yeshivah* say?"

The other student glared back at him. "The Gaon!"

Here Saadia Gaon, Sherira Gaon and Rav Hai Gaon had taught. Now Rabbi Shmuel, a scion of Shmuel the prophet, was Gaon.

The lecture came to an end and Rabbi Shmuel ben Eli descended from the dais, flanked by two servants. "Let us return to the palace."

Some of Rabbi Shmuel ben Eli's students entered the courtyard and gathered beneath a window above their heads. When the *Baal Hatosafos*, Rabbi Pesachia of Rotensburg, visited Baghdad, he was witness to the unusual lecture that now took place. Rabbi Shmuel had no sons but one daughter. And "she," Rabbi Pesachia reported, "is expert in *Tanach* and in Talmud. She gives instruction in *Tanach* to young men through a window. She herself is within the building, while the students are below outside and do not see her." (*Travels of R. Petachia*, p. 19)

Like a royal leader, Rabbi Shmuel ben Eli rode in a carriage back to his summer palace. The great reception room was hung with costly tapestry. Here, sixty servants served.

Rabbi Shmuel ben Eli glanced at the stack of letters that had arrived from Yemen, Damascus, Egypt—even from Russia.

He stepped up to his throne and sat down.

When Rabbi Shmuel ben Eli had become *rosh yeshivah* in 1164, the Yeshivah Gaon Yaakov had been losing influence. But Rabbi Shmuel ben Eli had strengthened the thousand-year-old *yeshivah* until he ruled *halachically* over all of Syria, Persia, Iraq and the land of Israel. In these countries, judges could be appointed only with his approval.

Although Rabbi Moshe ben Maimon was Chief Rabbi of Fostat, Rabbi Shmuel ben Eli's rule extended over Egypt.

Rabbi Shmuel ben Eli turned to the man standing next to him. "We were speaking yesterday of the *mishneh* Torah, which has recently arrived. The Chief Rabbi of Fostat writes there a *halachah* in complete contradiction to my understanding. Please take dictation. I wish my view to be known among all the Jews under my jurisdiction, so that no error be made."

Rabbi Shmuel dictated a proclamation regarding the *halachah* of sailing on a river on *Shabbos*. Rabbi Moshe ben Maimon had allowed such activity, in contradiction to the custom of Baghdad.

Rabbi Shmuel now reiterated his prohibition of sailing on *Shabbos*.

Soon, the public letter was distributed among the Jews of Baghdad. One of Rabbi Moshe's admirers wrote to Rabbi Moshe of this matter.

Rabbi Moshe replied, "You have said that these people defend their position, saying that it is a custom. Indeed, one must be very careful of a custom. But this is on condition that one knows that the matter is allowed, and one forbids it to oneself. But if people think that the matter is essentially forbidden, then they must be corrected." (*Igros*, p. 278)

There were many who feared that Rabbi Moshe's reputation would dim that of their *rosh yeshivah*, Rabbi Shmuel ben Eli. These people, who were not great Torah leaders, began a whispering campaign against Rabbi Moshe.

In Aleppo, Rabbi Zerachiah ben Berakhel, who would eventually marry Rabbi Shmuel's daughter, was collecting money for the Yeshivah Gaon Yaakov. He delivered a scathing attack on Rabbi Moshe's *Pirush Hamishnayos* and the *Mishneh Torah*.

Again, other lesser people took the opportunity to engage in personal attack.

Rabbi Moshe's student, Rabbi Yosef—now an outstanding *talmid chacham* in his own right—lived in Aleppo. In his anguish and anger at the attacks on his master's honor, Rabbi Yosef wrote heartfelt letters to Rabbi Moshe telling him of the slander and of how he had tried to defend Rabbi Moshe's honor.

Rabbi Moshe replied, "My son, my character traits are not like yours. I am already older and more experienced. I forgive the attacks on my honor. But you are unable to hold yourself back and suffer those incitements.

"I did not write the *Mishneh Torah* to become great in Israel or to gain a name, and so I am not distressed to hear that people are disparaging it.

"I wrote the *Mishneh Torah*—as Heaven knows—first of all for me, to make it easier to find what I needed and for my old age, and for the sake of Heaven, for I was zealous for the sake of Hashem, when I saw a nation without a true book of laws and without true, clear concepts. I did what I did solely for the sake of Heaven.

"I knew even as I wrote it that it would fall into the hands of jealous, evil-hearted people who would disparage it and claim that it is unnecessary or incomplete. I knew that it would fall into the hands of fools who would consider it unhelpful. I knew that it would fall into the hands of people who don't know how to learn, who confuse matters, who would be puzzled by passages in it because they don't know them well, or who would be unable to follow my conclusions.

"I knew that it would fall into the hands of people who believe themselves to be pious and who would attack its description of the fundamentals of Jewish faith.

"And these people constitute the majority.

"But I knew that it would also fall into the hands of those who would appreciate this work.

"You are the first of them. Even if I had no one but you, that would suffice for me.

"And how much happier am I that I have received a letter from the sages of France, who claim to be overwhelmed at what I have composed, and requesting that I send them a complete copy."

Rabbi Moshe went on to complain that there were people who, knowing little of Torah and interested in political intrigue, gossiped about him and tried to drag him down. "There are people who have no name and no standing and no ability, who have been overtaken by pride and jealousy."

Rabbi Zerachiah ben Berakhel and others now attacked Rabbi Moshe's *Pirush Hamishnayos*, because they did not realize that Rabbi Moshe had made many emendations in the text, based on versions of the texts by the Geonim.

"I do not claim that I have produced a flawless work," Rabbi Moshe admitted, "nor that I have never erred. To the contrary: whenever I have been corrected, I immediately corrected it." (*Igros Harambam*, *Shailat*, p. 306)

Rabbi Moshe was also thrust into an argument over the post of Exilarch.

The Exilarch had died and a new candidate for the post, Rabbi Shmuel (not Rabbi Shmuel ben Eli), asked Rabbi Moshe for his support.

"I received his letter," Rabbi Moshe wrote to Rabbi Yosef, "and I had it read in my house. And there were in the house all the people of Fostat, from small to great, since a *bris* was taking place, and it was *Sukkos*. This was a great day for [that rabbi]. The letter was read by Rabbi Shmuel the Teacher, while all the elders of the community stood to his right and left on the dais."

But Rabbi Moshe had unwittingly stepped into controversy, for Rabbi Shmuel ben Eli opposed Rabbi Shmuel's becoming Exilarch.

"I wrote to Rabbi Shmuel ben Eli, the *rosh yeshivah*, that if I had known that he was opposed to him, I would not have entered between them. But I had already acted, and it was known. I explained this to him and told him that it was impossible to retract."

In the midst of this exchange of letters, Rabbi Yosef told Rabbi Moshe about his plan to go to Baghdad and open a *yeshivah* there.

Rabbi Moshe replied, "I give you permission to open a study hall and learn and teach *halachah*, with the emphasis on knowing the *Mishneh Torah*. But I am afraid that you may be drawn into constant conflicts with others and achieve nothing but fighting.

"And also, if you need to teach, your business will cease. And I would not advise you to take from the students or their fathers. Earning a single *zuz* from being a tailor, carpenter or weaver is more beloved to me than the post of Exilarch.

"If you get paid by them, you shall be lowered, and if you

take from them, you shall be made contemptible.

"My advice is that you expend your energy on your business and on medicine, together with your dealing in Torah.

"And only teach the Rif, comparing his words with the *Mishneh Torah*. If you find a disagreement, study the appropriate *sugyos* to clarify the matter.

"But if you spend your time on commentaries dealing with the arguments of the *Gemara*, and those matters that I have already clarified, that is a waste of time and minimally useful." (*Igros Harambam*, Shailat, p. 312)

Rabbi Moshe closed his letter, "Do not stop writing to me. I have no better friend than your letters."

Now Rabbi Moshe wrote a few lines that reveal his personal warmth.

"Our friends all wish you good fortune. The elder, Abu Almaali [Rabbi Uziel] and his brother, and my nephew Abu Alrasa, and everyone in the house, including the servants, rejoice to hear good news from you and hope to again be together with you.

"Although our Sages have admonished us, 'One does not ask a man how his wife is doing' (*Kiddushin* 70b), a blessing is not forbidden. May both you and your wife have peace, and by next year, may you have a son."

19

The Guide to the Perplexed

CHAPTER BY CHAPTER, RABBI MOSHE SENT *DALALAT AL CHAIRIN—Moreh Nevuchim*—to Rabbi Yosef. In 1190, the great work was at last completed.

The age of philosophy has passed. Works of philosophy that once reached skyward like obelisks today appear as incomprehensible, arcane curiosities.

There was a time when philosophy defined how one understood the world. With logic and rationality, one investigated the greatest questions of life: Who is G-d? What is truth? What is reward and punishment?

Through philosophy, one defined the meaning of the world. One built an edifice of how the world works.

The Greeks had produced the greatest philosophers. The Moslem universities too were filled with theologians who taught complex and brilliant philosophies. But the Jewish intellectuals had no great philosophical edifice.

The Torah also provided answers to the deepest questions of life. But those who had studied the works of the gentile philosophers sought the same complexity of form in their study of the Torah. If the Torah contains everything, then it should as well contain philosophy.

Now Rabbi Moshe created his *Moreh Nevuchim*. His previous works had been meant for everyone. The *Moreh Nevuchim* was meant for a more exclusive reader. "It is not the purpose of this work to make itself totally understandable to the unlearned or to those who are only beginners in philosophy," Rabbi Moshe wrote in his introduction. "Nor is it meant for those who have engaged in no other study than that of Torah."

Then for whom was it? "This work is addressed to the religious man who believes completely in the validity of the Torah and whose belief is expressed throughout his being. Such a person must be complete in his religious obligations and character."

Yet this person—pious, learned, and of high character— had, as a sophisticated product of his day, engaged in learning philosophy. "He has studied the sciences of the philosophers and understood their works." And this had confused him. "But now he has felt distressed by the externals of the Torah. He is in a state of perplexity and confusion as to whether to follow his intellect."

Among some Jews intending to be pious, a simple-minded literalism regarding G-d's Being had spread. In a large city, a rabbi stood before his congregation. "We have heard from those who follow the paths of the Greeks or from those who have been drawn after the mystical Moslems that they believe that G-d is some kind of a non-physical Being. Heaven forfend! Do we not learn in the Torah and in the words of our Sages that G-d speaks, G-d raises His hand, G-d sheds tears that fall into the sea? Do our Sages not teach that G-d puts on *tefillin*? That He wraps Himself in a *tallis*?"

Rabbi Moshe wrote of such people, "I met a man who was considered one of the sages of Israel, and by the life of G-d, he knew *halachah* and knew the ins and outs of Talmudic discussion from his youth. He wondered whether G-d is a physical being, with an eye and hand and feet and internal organs, as the verses indicate, or if He is not physical.

"I have met other people from various lands who decided without any reservation that G-d is physical. They went so far as to declare that anyone who says the opposite is an unbeliever, calling him a heretic and an *apikores*.

"But these are the most foolish of people." (*Igeres Techias Hameisim*)

Rabbi Moshe intended to respond to such points of view in his work. "I propose to expound Biblical passages which have been impugned and to elucidate their hidden and true meaning which, when well-understood, serves as a means to remove the doubts concerning anything taught in *Tanach*."

Rabbi Moshe explained in *Moreh Nevuchim* (as well as in the *Pirush Hamishnayos* and in the *Mishneh Torah*) that the Torah is not always meant to be understood according to its superficial meaning. It often speaks allegorically. Like a veil worn by a princess, so do the images used by the Torah cover the beauty of the hidden meaning of the words.

Although meant for a small coterie of intellectual Jews, Rabbi Moshe's *Moreh Nevuchim* spread out among many people. Despite Rabbi Moshe's precautions, his work was also read by Moslem theologians. But Rabbi Moshe's fears that he would be harmed for his depiction of Moslem thought were not fulfilled. To the contrary, although Moslems argued with the *Guide*, they were deeply impressed.

There was a Muslim who walked alongside Rabbi Moshe like a shadow. Nine years before Rabbi Moshe's birth, he too had been born in Cordoba, Spain. Like Rabbi Moshe, he too came from a long line of distinguished scholars and jurists. His name was ibn Rushd (in Europe he was known as Averroes).

A Moslem theologian, he was also a physician. He composed the major Muslim philosophical works of his day, blending the teachings of Aristotle with his Moslem beliefs. His field of study was the Koran, and his claim was that the Koran must not be read literally, but interpreted allegorically according to the tools of reason.

Thus, the great debates in the Jewish world over the permissibility of the study of philosophy were mirrored in the Muslim world. Not only among Jews were books burned and banned. These great movements of passion had their analogues in the non-Jewish world, and ibn Rushd had his books both acclaimed and burned.

Thus, like wheels within wheels, the work of Rabbi Moshe and the dynamics of the Jewish communities were mirrored in the larger world of non-Jews and the concerns of non-Jewish thinkers.

In Yemen, a metalsmith came to the elder, Rabbi Nasanel ibn Alfayumi, father of Rabbi Yaakov, to whom Rabbi Moshe had addressed his famous *Igeres Teiman*. "My friends and I have been studying the words of the great Rabbi Moshe, and we are confounded. It seems that everything is a symbol. No simple meaning of any doctrine remains. Does Rabbi Moshe really believe in *techias hameisim*—the resurrection of the dead? Or does he claim that this, too, like the descriptions of G-d, is symbolic?"

When Rabbi Moshe received a letter on this from Yemen, he wrote back immediately, pointing out that he had in fact previously stated his belief in the resurrection as a basic tenet of Jewish belief.

Some scholars in Yemen forwarded a copy of this letter to Rabbi Shmuel ben Eli.

Rabbi Shmuel's face was grave as he read the letter. He turned to his assistant rabbi. "Remind me of the news that has arrived from Baghdad."

"Yes, Gaon Shmuel. A rabbi there has claimed on the basis of what he learned in Rabbi Moshe ben Maimon's *Mishneh Torah* that he does not believe in the resurrection."

How had the rafters of the synagogue shaken when that rabbi had made his declaration. "What! Does he deny a basic belief of Judaism? He is a heretic!"

But the rabbi had held up a manuscript. "Gentlemen, you may question me, but you certainly will not question the author of the *Mishneh Torah*!"

Rabbi Shmuel ben Eli set the letter down. "This Rabbi Moshe with his philosophical speculations will cause the greatest harm. I can see that some of his statements have been misunderstood. But others are simply not correct."

Rabbi Shmuel wrote an essay on the topic of the resurrection and sent some copies of it to Damascus, Yemen and Egypt.

When Rabbi Moshe read the contents of Rabbi Shmuel's letter, he realized that his belief in one of the basic principles of Judaism was being questioned. He was weary, overworked and beginning to gray. But he had to respond. His response to this letter, constituting his position on resurrection, has become known as the *Igeres Techias Hameisim—The Letter on Resurrection.*

"I declare," Rabbi Moshe wrote, "that the resurrection, which is well-known to our people, which is agreed upon by all factions, which is so often mentioned in the prayers composed by the prophets and greatest sages, which is discussed in the *Talmud* and *Midrash*, is a concept universally accepted by all Jews. The concept has no 'interpretation' at all. And if one has heard that a religious man has said the opposite, one may not believe such a report.

"Someone has claimed that I have said that the resurrection mentioned in *Tanach* is allegorical. But this is a clear falsehood and totally different from what I have actually said.

"It appears to me from the statements of our Sages that after people are resurrected, they will eat, drink, engage in marital relations, have children and die after a very long life, as will be in the days of the Mashiach. The life that has no death after it is the life of the World to Come, which is a life without physicality." (*Igros Harambam, Shailat*, p. 353)

But the attacks on Rabbi Moshe's views continued.

A middle-aged man named Yosef ibn Jabir returned home from the *yeshivah* one day shaken. Not even the sight of his children playing in the courtyard lifted his heart.

"Are all these criticisms made of Rabbi Moshe true?" he asked his wife, speaking more to himself than to her. "Must I abandon him?"

In a sharp-edged shadow that lay like a cool pool across the yard, his wife raised her hand to her head-covering and turned around in a lithe and automatic movement. "What do you mean, Yosef?"

"I am not a scholar. It is because Rabbi Moshe composed his *Pirush Hamishnayos* in Arabic that I have been able to begin learning the *mishneh*. But what do I say now that people are attacking Rabbi Moshe, claiming that he judges *halachah* incorrectly and that his basic beliefs are wrong?"

"You needed to learn the works of Rabbi Moshe when you began learning," ibn Jabir's wife said. "Perhaps now you have outgrown him."

"Yes, that is what everyone here seems to tell me," ibn Jabir said. "When I mention Rabbi Moshe's name in the synagogue, people look at me as though I had made a shocking statement. Today, a man who has been learning Torah all his life said to me, 'Rabbi Moshe ben Maimon has left the world of Torah values.'"

At that moment, Yosef ibn Jabir had felt as though he were being betrayed. He no longer saw the aquamarine and white mosaic on the wall of the synagogue, but flashed back to a memory of a bright summer day, when he was a small child and in the green field he danced home holding his first Hebrew book. Then there had been a rushing shadow, and the book had been ripped from his hands by an eight-year-old boy who ran off with it.

Now in the *beis midrash*, he heard this declaration of the other man with his stern voice, his face and arms stiff, as though he were a judge upon whose statements depended the validity of all things in the world. And Yosef ibn Jabir had felt again as though the Torah that he had begun to grasp was being taken away from him.

"Father, pick me up!" a little voice squealed.

The infant ran to Yosef, raising his small arms. With a smile, Yosef bent over and picked up the child.

"Are you good, my son?" he asked "Have you been learning your blessings?"

"Listen, Father: '*Baruch* . . . '"

In the evening, Yosef ibn Jabir wrote a letter to his great teacher.

Rabbi Moshe responded, "I have received the letter of the honored and precious student, Mr. Yosef. You say that you are an ignoramus. But I can see from your letter that you have toiled hard in learning Torah and have learned much of my *Pirush Hamishnayos*. You have mentioned that you heard from Torah sages in Baghdad comments against my statements. You wished to reply, and you have asked me to write you so that personal contact with me will help you learn. And I do so here.

"First of all, you must know that you are not an ignoramus but my student and my beloved one.

"I regard anyone as my student, even if he understands

only one verse or one *halachah*, whether he learned it in the holy tongue or in Arabic or Aramaic, as long as he attempts to understand the Torah in any language.

"The main thing is learning Torah.

"But if a person never learned, there applies to him the verse, 'He has despised the word of G-d.' (*Bamidbar* 15:31) If a person used to learn but has grown lax, even if he is a great sage, he violates the positive commandment of learning Torah, which is equal to everything else.

"Do not insult yourself, and do not give up hoping to attain perfection.

"The greatest sages began learning when they were already grown, and look what they achieved.

"Try to learn the holy tongue until you can understand the *Mishneh Torah* in the holy tongue in which I composed it. It is easy to understand and to use. After you practice on one volume, you will understand the entire work.

"I have no interest in translating it into Arabic, because it would lose in the translation.

"In fact, I am now involved with arranging a translation of the *Pirush Hamishnayos* and the *Sefer Hamitzvos* into the holy tongue.

"You say that you have heard people say that I deny the resurrection. This is a terrible slander."

After addressing these and other issues, Rabbi Moshe concluded, "I have been told—perhaps it is true, perhaps not—that there is a man who speaks evil of me, who speaks to gain honor at the expense of my humiliation, and that he has spoken disparagingly of my *Mishneh Torah*.

"I heard that you responded to him and answered him back. Do not do this.

"I forgive anyone who does anything out of foolishness, and how much more if he has some personal gain. It does not hurt me.

"In fact, we both gain. He is regarded by others as a wise man, for he is arguing with someone that others rely on. This helps him in this world.

"And it helps me in both this world and the World to Come. It is self-understood that it helps me in the World to Come. It also keeps me in this world, because when people want to hide that which G-d has revealed, it becomes even more revealed.

"But besides this, you are bringing useless strife and conflict upon yourself.

"I do not ask help from anyone. I leave every man to what he desires for himself."

A gust of laughter swept through the *beis midrash* when Yosef ibn Jabir read Rabbi Moshe's letter aloud.

"Rabbi Moshe addressed a *halachic* response to an ignoramus like you! That *really* shows what level he is on."

In the *yeshivah* of Rabbi Yosef ben Yehudah, the noisome insults were like an enfilade. This *yeshivah* was the outpost of Rabbi Moshe's methodology. Here, under the *rosh yeshivah* who was himself a student of Rabbi Moshe, students learned from and venerated the works of Rabbi Moshe.

When Rabbi Yosef entered the study hall, a group of teenaged students, hot with the insult to the *gadol hador*, surrounded their *rosh yeshivah*.

"Rebbe, we heard someone say . . ."

"Rebbe, So-and-So has made fun of . . ."

Rabbi Yosef remained silent until the students' angry outcries faded to silence.

"It is an outrage!" Rabbi Yosef at last replied. "But what can I say? Rabbi Moshe ben Maimon is the master. This is a matter that concerns him, and it is up to him to decide what will be done."

Again, Rabbi Moshe received a letter from his beloved student, filled with the calumnies that people were flinging.

This was a new charge against him: that he replied to the letter of a simple man!

"Know," Rabbi Moshe replied, "that I intend to do whatever is humble, even if it causes me great damage in the eyes of the public. Whoever wants to show his perfection at the expense of my imperfection, even if he is the smallest of students—I forgive him for it."

Rabbi Moshe now dealt with Rabbi Yosef's hot feelings. Rabbi Moshe revealed that in younger years, he too would enter into *halachic* arguments with a militant spirit, eager to vanquish his opponent.

"You are still young," wrote Rabbi Moshe. "When you see people saying misleading things and spreading falsehoods, your age causes you to feel anguish and anger.

"I too was your age. I too had feelings as strong as yours, and even stronger.

"You must have heard about the time I argued with Rabbi Yehudah Hakohen ben Pirchon regarding two questions on *kashrus*. And there was the argument I had with Judge Sijilmasah [a city in Morocco] regarding a divorce; and the argument between me and Avi Yosef ben Yosef regarding a captive woman, and many other such cases.

"With my speaking and with my writings, I would make my friends rejoice and my opponents weep!" (*Igros Harambam*)

There was another aspect to this controversy. Rabbi Moshe was highly respected by the Moslem clerics. Were they to be persuaded that Rabbi Moshe disbelieved in doctrines held by the Moslems, such as the resurrection, he might lose his position—perhaps even his life.

Rabbi Moshe's self-control and mature sense of perspective helped him guide his way through this thicket of controversy.

"In these times," Rabbi Moshe wrote ruefully, "if a person

decides to do or say everything in reaction to what others do, he will only cleave to evil, since most people whom he will see are not straight. A person who wishes to be mature should look to improve his own qualities and intellectual abilities, and not concern himself with foolishness." (*Igros Harambam*, *Shailat:*, p. 421)

20

More Controversy

IN 1191, THE TWO-YEAR SIEGE BY RICHARD THE LION-HEARTED against Acco resulted in a victory that caused the death of tens of thousands of Moslems.

Over a hundred thousand Crusaders took part in that siege. Almost half of them died from disease and battle.

Saladin again was in despair. Now that the Christians controlled the port, they would march against Jerusalem and take it back.

In September, 1191, Richard again attacked Saladin and beat him back.

Saladin destroyed the walls of Ashkelon and the town of Yaffa so that the Christians could not use them.

The Christians were coming closer to Jerusalem. Frantically, Saladin destroyed towns, razed castles, burned farms and poisoned all the wells.

His strategy worked. Richard the Lion-Hearted realized that without the resources of the countryside, a siege of Jerusalem would result in the loss of thousands of Christian lives.

To the disgust of his French allies, who were filled with religious fervor to regain the holy city, he engineered a truce with Saladin in June of 1192.

As Richard spoke with one of Saladin's subalterns, the man boasted of the greatness of Egypt. "We have there one of the finest physicians in the entire world," the man said. "He is a Jew, but he is more learned and able than any other of the Sultan's physicians."

"Oh yes?" Richard the Lion-Hearted said. "What is his name?"

"He is called Moshe ben Maimon. He is the Chief Rabbi of the Jews of Fostat."

Richard merely nodded his head. But the next morning, he dispatched a messenger to Fostat.

Rabbi Moshe was coming home from his duties at the palace of the vizier. He was worn-out. So hard did he work, so many long hours did he have to put into his work that he had almost no time left to learn Torah.

If medicine were only a profession that required no thought and no responsibility, his work would be easier. But he needed to review the material.

As he arrived at Fostat, the sun had already set behind the deep blue horizon. With utter weariness, Rabbi Moshe slipped down from the donkey he had ridden and walked into the city.

Rabbi Moshe described his circumstances to his student Rabbi Yosef: "I have become very famous as a physician among the political leaders, such as the judges, the emirs and the Vizier Alfatzil and other political leaders. But I get paid nothing.

"As for the common people—I am removed from them,

and they have no way to get to me.

"This causes me to lose my entire day in Cairo visiting the ill. When I come to Fostat, it is already night. I only have time to review my books of medicine. You know how long it takes to learn this profession, how difficult it is for a person who is responsible and careful and who doesn't want to say anything without being sure and how to draw correct conclusions.

"As a result, I don't have time to study Torah. I am only able to learn on *Shabbos*. As for other topics, I have no time to study them at all. This really hurts me." (*Igros Harambam*)

In one of the innumerable rooms that lined the honeycombed structure of the palace, Said ben Sana Almulk pulled aside the brocaded silk curtain and gazed into the courtyard below him. The sky was studded with blazing stars. In the courtyard, a group of courtiers was singing melancholy songs whose beauty made his heart ache. It had been—how long?—only three days since he had lain on his couch, sick unto death, persuaded that he had cast away his life on dissolution.

But the physician, Rabbi Moshe ben Maimon, had completely cured him with a wise prescription of herbs, diet and exercise. The rhythmic strumming of the *oud* and the jingling tambourine enlivened him, and words of praise and gratefulness to the physician sprang up in him. Quickly, lest he lose the inspiration, Almulk went to his desk and jotted down a poem of praise:

Galen's art heals only the body,
But Abu Amran's [Rabbi Moshe's] heals the body and soul.
His knowledge has made him the physician of the century.
With his wisdom, he could heal the sickness of ignorance.
Were he to attend to the moon,
He would free her of her spots when she is full,
He would heal her of her periodic defects,
And at the time of her weakness save her from waning.

Late into the night, the courtiers played music and recited poetry until they drifted away, and the songs that had rung in the courtyard faded into silence.

On his couch, Almulk slept even as the sun rose like an aureole and transformed itself into a blazing, white inferno.

The shimmering dawn found the messenger of Richard the Lion-Hearted already driving hard down the length of the Nile. At the same time, Rabbi Moshe was again riding upon his donkey to Cairo. To his right rose the half-completed Citadel. The walls surrounding the area were now thirty feet high and ten feet thick. In the center of the complex stood the fortress.

Thousands of workers were constructing the walls and round towers from which soldiers would be able to shoot down at enemy soldiers trying to scale the walls.

Within the Citadel, workers were breaking a tunnel through solid rock that would reach to the Nile and provide the Citadel with an independent supply of drinking water. Eventually, the tunnel was almost three hundred feet long, and broad enough to contain a ramp for the animals that powered the machinery lifting the water.

"Rabbi Moshe ben Maimon?"

Rabbi Moshe looked up. It was an outlandishly-dressed man with a pale face and, under his mail hood, straw-colored hair. His accent was strange as well.

"Yes, I am he."

"I come as a representative of Richard the Lion-Hearted, King of England. His highness offers you the honor of becoming his personal physician."

Weeks later, the messenger's wife, Lady Juliet of Dombrowster, repeated the story to her friends as her husband had told it to her. "And then wouldn't you all know it," she exclaimed, her curly golden hair bouncing as she spoke with spirit, "the Jewish rabbi refused the offer of King

Richard! He said he wants to 'remain with his community.'
Well—a Jew, and an Arab Jew at that—there's no telling what
a man like that can be thinking!"

A few months later, in October of 1192, Richard the Lion-
Hearted returned to England.

Saladin's heart filled with joy. The land of Israel now was
his.

Saladin returned to his palace in Damascus and planned
his pilgrimage to Mecca, the holiest Moslem site, where each
Moslem must go at least one time in his lifetime. But on March
4, 1193, after a short illness, Saladin died. He was fifty-five
years old.

A mixture of cruelty and nobility, Saladin had given away
all his personal possessions to charity. The money he left
behind was not even enough to pay for his grave.

One of Saladin's sons, Alaziz, now became sultan of Egypt.
His brother, Alfadal, became his senior administrator.

On the day of Alaziz's accession to the throne, guests
reclined in the courtyards of the crowded palace, "among
thornless lote-trees, clustered plantains and spreading shade,
with water gushing and fruit in plenty, neither out of reach
nor forbidden." (*Sura* 56)

In an inner chamber, a musician sat playing an Arab lute
with a long neck, whose music tinkled like crystal water and
pulsed with a throb of loneliness and excitement. The strings
of the lute were dyed yellow, red, white and black, corresponding to the four humors in the body: yellow bile, blood,
mucous and black bile.

Before the musician sat a tall, thin man in the robes of a
prince, his head leaning forward, his eyes dull. Another young
man swept into the room, flanked by older men at his side, in
crimson and purple robes.

"Alafdal!" said Alaziz. "Are you despondent today?"

Alafdal gave a weak smile. "My brother, is this not the most happy day of my life, to see you placed upon the throne of Egypt? But the doctors have prescribed for me music every afternoon to treat my depression."

"Come!" said Alaziz. "The ceremony is about to begin, and the notables await our entry."

He took Alafdal by the shoulders and bussed his cheeks. Now the two men stepped into the corridor and a whisper ran through the halls: "Alaziz is coming—the new sultan!"

Hours later, Rabbi Moshe walked with a stooped, heavy step to his door. He had endured the endless inauguration party at the palace and now he might have some few hours' rest. As he passed a courtyard, a door opened and two men came out, arm in arm. Behind them, Rabbi Moshe heard the Arab lute, the beat of drums and the voice of a woman singing inappropriate songs in the modern Arab fashion. She was joined by a chorus of men.

A slit for a *mezuzah* was carved into the doorpost. Jews were singing such songs!

Rabbi Moshe entered the gate.

"This is a private party, sir"—the servant at the door interrupted himself—"oh, Rabbi Moshe!" He stood back and allowed Rabbi Moshe to pass by him.

As Rabbi Moshe entered the courtyard, the guests tapped each other and stood up in respect. The woman stopped singing, and the lute ceased to play.

Rabbi Moshe said in a tired voice, "I am surprised at you! To play such music! This is not the way of Jews." The musician twanged a string by accident, and its note hung in the stillness, and then faded.

"What kind of joy is this? And listening to a woman sing! That is outrageous. We are a holy people. Whatever a Jew does must be for the purpose of perfecting himself."

"Then may we never play music?"

"One may sing praises to G-d." (*Igros Harambam*)

214

The woman singer had slipped away. Rabbi Moshe turned and walked out of the courtyard, into the dark, baffled passageway.

A man walked alongside Rabbi Moshe, carrying an oil lamp. "Allow me!" he declared.

Behind him, in the courtyard, one of the men murmured, "I had no idea that Rabbi Moshe is so old."

"That is the wonder!" the man next to him replied. "He is no more than fifty-five years old. Yet he has worn himself out."

When Rabbi Moshe returned home, a line of patients was waiting to see him. He sighed. Again he would have no chance to learn Torah.

By the time the last patient left, it was after midnight. Lying in bed, he picked up a letter he had received a number of months before. He had been too weary and sometimes too ill to respond earlier.

There was a knock at the door. "What is it?" Rabbi Moshe asked.

A servant entered. When he saw Rabbi Moshe lying on the bed, too tired to raise his head from the pillow, he began to retreat.

"What did you want?"

"The *dayan*, Rabbi Yitzchak, has been waiting all evening to see you. I will ask him to come back—"

"No, I'll see him now."

Rabbi Yitzchak came in. He walked up to Rabbi Moshe and took Rabbi Moshe's hand between his. "Rabbi Moshe, you are overworked. You cannot continue like this."

Rabbi Moshe shook his head back and forth on the pillow.

"I'll come back tomorrow," Rabbi Yitzchak said.

"Tomorrow will only be the same. Tell me what you came to discuss."

Rabbi Yitzchak pulled out from his tunic the section of Damages—*Nezikin*—from the *Mishneh Torah*. He turned through the pages. "Here it is!" He put the page before Rabbi Moshe's eyes. "Please read this *halachah*."

Rabbi Moshe read the words. "What question do you have?"

"What is the source of this *halachah*?"

"The source?" Rabbi Moshe thought a moment. "Go to the shelf and take down *Mesechte Yevamos*."

Rabbi Yitzchak brought the heavy volume to Rabbi Moshe. Rabbi Moshe flipped through the pages. He turned the volume to Rabbi Yitzchak. "The *halachah* is mentioned here in passing."

Rabbi Yitzchak's face lit up. "Excellent!"

Amatziah entered the room with a tray on which were two glasses of aromatic water, sweetened with honey.

Rabbi Moshe took a glass from the tray. Making a blessing, he sipped at the liquid. "If G-d grants me the strength, I would like to compose a companion work to the *Mishneh Torah*, citing all the sources of the *halachos*, particularly those *halachos* that are not found in their place in the *Gemara*. This will be a great undertaking." (*Igros Harambam, Shailat*, p. 444)

(Rabbi Moshe did not compose this work. However, other commentators have cited the sources, chief among them, Rabbi Yosef Kairo in his *Kesef mishneh*.)

"Go to sleep, Rabbi Moshe."

"Good night, Rabbi Yitzchak. I shall see you in the morning."

Alone in the shadowy room, Rabbi Moshe read the letter he had received.

He recalled the letter's author, Rabbi Pinchas ben Rabbi Meshuallam. Years before, he had come from Provence, France, to learn from Rabbi Moshe. Since then, he had moved to Alexandria and become a *dayan*. And now he had written a letter! Rabbi Moshe glanced at the date. It had been written long months before. But how could he answer, when he was so ill and weary?

In Alexandria, Rabbi Pinchas wrote in the letter, a number of Jews had risen against him. "How can you teach such strange *halachos*? What strange things have you been taught by your teacher, Rabbi Moshe?"

Rabbi Pinchas had shifted beneath his robe. "I teach you the clear *halachah* as I learned it from my teacher."

"We have a tradition from our forefathers that if a Jew is ritually unclean," one man declared "he must bathe before praying. But you wish to say that he is allowed to enter the synagogue and pray and read from the Torah."

"We will denounce you to the other judges!" another Jew cried out.

In the stifling atmosphere of the synagogue, Rabbi Pinchas had stood mute, defeated. Another man attacked as well. "And what sort of *sefer* is the *Mishneh Torah*? Does your rabbi think so highly of himself that he wishes to take the place of the Talmud? He himself writes in his introduction that this is his purpose!"

The sky outside the window was yellow and sickly. What did these people want from him? Rabbi Pinchas wiped a broad sleeve against the film of perspiration on his forehead. "I will submit your questions . . ."

Now in his bedroom, Rabbi Moshe slowly dipped a quill into a glazed inkwell and wrote his response to Rabbi Pinchas's letter. "To the great *dayan*, the strong fortress, the wondrous sage.

"I only delayed answering your previous letters because of illness, not because of anything bad that I heard about you, for I do not listen to slander. I know that when anything is repeated, things are changed and added.

"Who are these people who rose against you, 'the entire people, elders and the young'? They were only a handful, the ignoramuses and fools! And yet you treated their words as though they are great sages, and receivers of a great tradition from their forefathers.

"As for the *Mishneh Torah*, you must first of all be aware that I did not say, Heaven forbid, that one should not learn *Gemara*, the Rif or other such authorities. He Who knows all is my witness that I have for about a year and a half only taught my *Mishneh Torah* to two or three people who learned a few volumes. But most of my students wished to learn the Rif. I taught them all the *halachos* a few times. Besides this, two students asked to learn the *Gemara*, and I taught them the *mesechtos* that they requested.

"Did I ever command, or did it ever occur to me, to burn all the *sefarim* that were composed before my work? I said clearly at the beginning of my work that I only composed it because of people's lack of application. It is meant for a person who cannot descend to the depth of the Talmud and cannot understand from the Talmud what is forbidden and what is allowed.

"My work is different. Others have preceded me and composed works giving *halachic* decisions in Hebrew and Arabic on specific topics. But since Rabbi Yehudah Hanasi, author of the *mishneh*, and those of his company, no one has given *halachic* decisions regarding the entire Talmud and all the laws of the Torah.

"One reason I had for not citing sources was that giving *halachos* in the name of the sages who stated them would have encouraged the Karaites, who would have said that the sage made up the *halachah*.

"As for my calling you an angry person—it is true that I said that. But do not feel bad. Our Sages teach us that 'when a scholar gets angry, it is the Torah that caused it.' As the verse says, 'Are not my words like fire? says Hashem.'" (*Yirmiyahu* 23:29; *Taanis* 4a)

"I must answer your letters briefly. I am very busy on many matters. My body is weak, and I am not even able to read letters, how much more am I unable to answer them, unless they are questions regarding wisdom. And I have no free time, for my body is constantly weary, and I am teaching myself various topics." (*Igros Harambam*)

There was another rabbi from Provence who now also served as *dayan* in Alexandria. His name was Rabbi Antoli ben Rabbi Yosef.

"All the judges of Alexandria or most of them come before me," Rabbi Moshe once wrote. (*Igros*) They told Rabbi Antoli of Rabbi Moshe's greatness. Rabbi Antoli never visited Rabbi Moshe, but they exchanged letters.

"The Exalted Lord knows," Rabbi Moshe wrote in one letter to Rabbi Antoli, "that because of my great love for you, I wrote these lines, although I am sick and overwhelmed day and night, for I have no spare time. But I was afraid that I might be suspected of being proud, so I troubled myself to write, and may I be granted compassion from Heaven."

The rabbis in Montpellier in southern France sat in excited conversation over the chapters of Rabbi Moshe's writings that had reached them.

One of the rabbis summed up the feelings of the others. "For so long, I have had many questions about what the Torah requires us to believe and not to believe. And yet I have not had anyone that would even listen to my questions."

Another rabbi said, "When I was growing up, whenever I had a question, I was suspected of doubting what the Torah says!"

"Yes, I know about that," said a third rabbi.

"Now I can at last read a work dealing with the questions about faith that have long simmered in my heart: free will, divine providence, astrology. I remember that when I used to ask such questions, my teacher would tell me, 'This isn't the type of question that the Sages would ask.' Now I have at last found a great teacher who not only asks the same questions that have occupied me my whole life, but also answers them."

Together, the rabbis wrote a letter to Rabbi Moshe, asking him his views on a number of topics, particularly astrology.

Rabbi Moshe wrote back, "Know, my masters, that I have examined these matters thoroughly. People claim that from astrology one may know the future of a country or a person for the rest of his life. I learned everything there is to know about astrology. It seems to me that I read every single work on the topic written in or translated into Arabic. I read every word, understood it and grasped it to the very depths.

"Know, my masters, that all the predictions based on astrology are not words of wisdom at all, but foolishness!"

21

Medical Responsibilities

"WHEN YOU RECLINE TO SLEEP, THE MUSICIAN SHOULD PLAY ON THE lute and sing for an hour. Then he should lower his voice gradually, and play more softly until you fall asleep. Physicians and philosophers have stated that when the melody of the strings induces sleep, the psyche is endowed with a good nature and broadened, thereby improving its management of the body."

Alafdal lay on the white, silk-embroidered couch, eating pistachio nuts from an iridescent salver. He was reading the medical words authored by Rabbi Moshe. Before him, in the air that had been sprayed with musk, a fountain tinkled melodiously and servants in impeccable white stood at rapt attention.

Half a year had passed since Alafdal's brother, Sultan Alaziz, had died. Now, after his mourning and months of turmoil, Alafdal had become ruler of all Egypt: Vizier Alafdal. Yet he was still ill and unsettled. Foreboding paled his face, and in his mouth, he tasted bitterness. He was a thin man of thirty with intense eyes that stared forward morosely.

He had grown up on the battlefield. He had learned to drink hard and had sought the most dissolute pleasures.

Now, after a year of vicious maneuvering and fighting, he had emerged as the inheritor of the throne. Yet his problems had not decreased.

He asked an advisor, "Who is the greatest physician of the court?"

"It is a Jew, your highness."

"He shall be my personal physician."

He had written the humbling lines—sent in the strictest confidence—to Rabbi Moshe. He suffered, he confided, from difficulty in his bowel movements and a feeble digestion, as well as from depression, evil thoughts and fear of death.

Rabbi Moshe had written two works for the vizier, entitled *The Regimen of Health* and *The Causes of Symptoms*. Now Vizier Alafdal reread these short works. "If a patient can be treated with a measure of nourishment alone, he should not be treated with medication . . ."

"Vizier."

Alfadal looked up. It was his old friend Shajar. "Yes," he said in a dreary voice. "What is it?"

"I have come at your bidding. You requested my company that I may tell you stories and make you laugh."

Afadal sat up and forced himself to smile. "Thank you, Shajar." He swung up from the couch and clapped his friend on the shoulder. His eyes brightened. "But actually, now that you're here, I have something else that I wish to talk to you about.

"You know the interest that I have taken in the welfare of my subjects. You know that I have spent money on the support of the poor, that I have opened schools and done what I could to improve the economy of the populace.

"And you know about my interest in finding antidotes for poisons." He went on to tell his friend about different cases of poisoning.

Meanwhile, in a courtyard in Fostat, an old man rocked his baby granddaughter. The girl's young mother stood at the kitchen counter, cutting gourds. There was an outcry from the courtyard. She ran out to the old man, who was clutching at his foot.

"What is it?" cried the woman. Then she saw a thick-bodied, golden Egyptian cobra slithering into a hole at the base of the wall.

Elsewhere, a late party-reveler in the northern quarter of Cairo crawled into bed. A black centipede, seven inches long, dropped out of the bedsheet onto his leg, and dug its poisonous pincers into his thigh. Looking down, the man leaped up in disgust, flinging away the noisome insect. But a hot pain was already radiating through his body.

In the Red Sea, a ten-year-old boy dove to the sea floor from a ragged *dhow*. Here the light was mysterious and soft, and schools of brilliant golden and crimson fish flickered past. He scrabbled amidst the oyster bed, putting the oysters most likely to contain pearls into a bag at his waist.

Then he pushed against the sandy bottom and leaped upward. His left foot pressed against a bottom-dwelling fish whose raised poisoned bristles penetrated his foot.

When the boy reached the surface of the sea, he gasped and cried out, "My foot is burning! Pull me in!"

And there were the thousands of bee stings, spider bites and bites from the packs of wild dogs that roamed the outskirts of the cities, infected with rabies.

Alafdal continued telling Shajar, "I ordered the physicians to store up the most potent poison antidotes we have: theriac for poisoning and snakebite, and the mithridate electuary."

"I know," said Shajar. "A number of ministers complained because you spent so much money importing the ingredients for these antidotes from India and other lands."

"Yes," said Alafdal. "And now the supply has been almost entirely used up. I have ordered more, but obviously something less expensive must be done. Besides that, by the time someone can actually get to a physician, it is often too late. We need inexpensive antidotes that people can use right away."

"Cannot the physicians devise other, less expensive remedies—"

"Come now, Shajar, you know that most of the physicians in Egypt are not fit to—"

"But what about Abu Amran Musa?"

Alafdal thought a moment and nodded his head. Clapping Shajar on the back, he said, "That's it!"

The next day, when Rabbi Moshe rode home on his donkey from the vizier's palace, a thin film of ribbed clouds stretched across the sky. Gazing at the dull dust and pebbles of the road, Rabbi Moshe reviewed the directive that the vizier had given him.

"I order you to write a concise manual of first aid for poisons, naming the means of healing and nourishment and enumerating some general antidotes."

The work that Rabbi Moshe began to work on that evening was the *Treatise on Poison and Their Antidotes*. This extraordinary monograph became one of Rabbi Moshe's most famous medical works. He was the first to distinguish between the two types of major poisons: the neurotoxins (in viper poison, paralyzing the victim) and the hemolyns (in adder poison, causing hemorrhaging and fever). This discovery went largely unnoted until it was rediscovered in the early part of the nineteenth century.

The range of Rabbi Moshe's knowledge about all sorts of

poisons was astonishing. His wide variety of techniques on how to treat them are still in use to this day. And his knowledge of antidotes and the precision of his measurement of ingredients are remarkable.

Rabbi Moshe devoted a section of his treatise to dealing with deliberate poisoning. Such passages, as well as the jealousy that others in the royal palace bore him, gave rise to various stories about Rabbi Moshe being poisoned by his enemies and then healing himself. (The information culled here was taken from *The Medical Writings of Moses Maimonides*, Volume Two, Suessman Muntner, editor.)

Rabbi Moshe continued his demanding schedule. In the realm of medicine, he wrote his *Medical Aphorisms*, one of his most enduring medical works.

Rabbi Moshe's *Aphorisms* were reminiscent of the *Mishneh Torah* in their organization. Just as the *Mishneh Torah* had compartmentalized the great mass of knowledge in the Talmud, so did the *Aphorisms* arrange the sayings of Galen, the classical physician.

In this work, Rabbi Moshe made remarkable observations on a wide range of medical topics, many of them centuries ahead of their time.

He described the circulation of the blood—a description that would not surface again until five centuries later.

In Chapter Twenty-Five of this work, Rabbi Moshe took issue with the classical physician, Galen, on over seventy points.

In Rabbi Moshe's day, the word of Galen was taken by the majority of physicians to be irrefutably true. Complex defenses were made of his patently false comments.

But Rabbi Moshe wrote, "No one is without fault save the prophets."

In Rabbi Moshe's day, the ancients—Aristotle, Galen and others—were assumed to have mastered all knowledge. If any new evidence were found that contradicted them, the new evidence was disregarded or explained away.

Roger Bacon is credited with having discarded this approach, replacing it with the modern scientific method based on observation and experiment.

But Bacon was preceded by centuries by Rabbi Moshe. In his *Aphorisms*, Rabbi Moshe wrote, "If any man declares to you that he has found facts that he has observed and confirmed with his own experience, even if you consider this man to be most trustworthy and highly authoritative, be cautious in accepting what he says to you. If he attempts to persuade you to accept his opinion or any doctrine that he believes in, think critically and understand what he means. Investigate and weigh this opinion or that hypothesis according to the requirements of pure logic, without paying attention to his contention that he affirms from his own observations." (*Aphorisms* 25:69)

"Help! The doctor has collapsed!"

Two servants rushed into Rabbi Moshe's examining room. The great sage lay motionless on the floor, his breathing shallow and unsteady.

They picked him up gently and laid him down on the examining couch.

A woman appeared at the door. Then she rushed into the room.

"My husband!" She turned to the servants with a look of appeal. "Is he all right?"

The patients crowded in the examining room chattered excitedly.

"You stay here and keep the patients out," the oldest servant said. "I'll go get a doctor."

For years, Rabbi Moshe had driven himself to the point of exhaustion. Every morning, he had left the house before dawn and remained up until midnight or one or two in the morning, eating only one meal a day. At last, his body had collapsed.

Avraham came home in the evening from the *beis midrash*. He was eleven years old.

To his dismay, the examining room was empty. He ran into the house. "Where is Father?" he called out.

His mother turned to him. Her eyes were red, her cheeks blotched. "Your father is not well, son. He is resting now."

"Is he . . . ?"

The question hung unfinished for a few moments.

His mother forced a smile. "Do not worry, Avraham. G-d will do what is best."

On his bed, Rabbi Moshe slept, his pale, wrinkled hands on top of the coverlet.

For almost a year, Rabbi Moshe remained in bed.

When at last he arose on shaky legs and stepped into his courtyard, he was a physically diminished man. "Today, I am like a sick person who is out of danger," Rabbi Moshe wrote. "Most of the day, I lie in bed. I am not today as I was in the days of my youth. My power has gone. My heart is weakened and my breath shortened. My tongue is heavy, and my hand shakes so that I refrain even from writing a short letter." (*Igros*)

"Why do they come here?" his wife asked one day. In the reception room, Moslem men and women, some of whom had travelled from afar, were crowded together. "Why do they bother you? Why must you visit the vizier and write medical works? You do not have one hour to yourself!"

"What can I do?" her husband replied. "Now that I have become famous, the yoke of the gentiles has fallen on my neck."

"I do not understand," she said. She fell silent.

"What is it?"

"You of all people were made for a life devoted entirely to

Torah. What has happened?"

"This has been G-d's Will, and I accept it," Rabbi Moshe replied. "But I do have my regrets about how I have chosen to spend my time on the Sciences.

"I want you to know, my dear wife, that before I was born, the Torah made itself known to me. Before I was born, the Torah sanctified me to learn it. I was placed in this world to spread the wellsprings of the Torah.

"The Torah has been the great passion of my life. From my youngest days, I have taken pleasure in her.

"Yet I took other 'wives'—the wisdoms of the other nations—foreign women who became the rivals of the Torah.

"G-d knows that I only wanted these sciences to serve my Torah learning. I meant them to be the Torah's perfumers, cooks and bakers.

"I hoped that with my scientific abilities, I would be able to show the nations and their princes the beauty of the Torah, for the Torah is very beautiful.

"Yet what happened? My time spent on learning Torah decreased, for my time has been so divided on so many divisions of the sciences." (*Igros*)

In Lunel, in the south of France, the sky hung like a violet curtain above the cluster of white houses, their orange-red tiled roofs visible across fields of scrub and yellow blossoms.

Rabbi Yehonasan Hakohen sat at the head of the table in the *beis midrash*. "You will recall that a few years ago, we sent a few letters to the great sage, Rabbi Moshe of Egypt."

"Yes, that's right," said another rabbi. "Has he at last replied?" He gazed at the manuscript that lay on the table before Rabbi Yehonasan.

"Has he sent the translation of his *Moreh Nevuchim*?" someone else echoed.

Rabbi Yehonasan lifted up a letter. "Rabbi Moshe apologizes in his letter for having taken so long to answer. He says that he was deathly ill."

In Fostat, Rabbi Moshe, lying back in bed, had dictated to his secretary, "Do not be upset that I am not sending you this letter in my own hand. I have not had the time, since I am weak and enfeebled."

Rabbi Moshe recalled when he had first read Rabbi Yehonasan's letter. Such astute questions he had received regarding his *Mishneh Torah*! This was why he had written the *Mishneh Torah*: to communicate with other people—intelligent and appreciative people.

Rabbi Moshe dictated, "I, Moshe, tell you, Rabbi Yehonasan Hakohen, that when I received your letter and your questions, I rejoiced greatly. I said to myself, 'Praise G-d, Who has not withheld a redeemer.'

"I knew that my words had reached someone who knew their content, understood their hidden meanings and who could discuss them intelligently.

"I told myself, 'This will console you and sustain you in your old age.'

"All the questions that you asked, you asked well. Every query that you posed, you posed well. Do not fear, for I am with you, I am today replying to each of your questions."

Sitting about the table in Lunel, Rabbi Yehonasan read Rabbi Moshe's words aloud.

One of the rabbis asked, "Did he send the *Dalalat Haririn* translated into Hebrew, as we asked him to?"

Rabbi Yehonasan patted the manuscript. "These are the first two parts of the *Dalalat Haririn*—in Arabic." He looked down the table at a Sephardi rabbi. "Rabbi Shmuel . . . ?"

Rabbi Shmuel ibn Tibbon cleared his throat. "If you wish, I will undertake a translation of the work."

The following day, Rabbi Shmuel ibn Tibbon began his work on the *Dalalat Haririn*. He translated exactingly, eager to transmit Rabbi Moshe's thought precisely. But he began having to mark passages and phrases about whose meaning he was uncertain.

"This is more than a private translation," Rabbi Yehonasan told Rabbi ibn Tibbon. "Your work will benefit all Ashkenazi Jews. Write to Rabbi Moshe, and present him with your questions. Perhaps he will respond."

Rabbi Shmuel ibn Tibbon walked home in the evening, his head filled with exciting thoughts. He had set down all his questions in a letter. But now he thought that perhaps he would travel and sit before the feet of the great rabbi. A ghostly half moon shone in the pale afternoon sky.

In Fostat, Rabbi Moshe heard through the window the yelling of the camel drivers jostling tens of camels to the slaughterhouse.

He had escaped to this solitary room to respond to the letter that Rabbi Shmuel ibn Tibbon had sent him. In his great weariness, Rabbi Moshe leaned against the wall as he wrote. But even this did not suffice him, and he tottered over to the bed, where he continued to write in a frail handwriting. (*Igros Harambam, Shailat*, p. 550)

"It is certainly fitting for you to undertake this translation," Rabbi Moshe wrote. "The Creator has given you an understanding heart to comprehend allegory and figures of speech. I see that you have descended to the depth of the matter and have revealed the hidden secrets.

"You mention that you would like to come here. You will be welcome. My joy to see you will be greater than your joy in seeing me.

"But you will have to travel in danger across the sea. And so I must advise you not to endanger yourself, for when you do arrive, you will only be able to look at me. I will give you as much honor as I can. But do not expect that you will be able to spend as little as an hour with me, day or night.

"The matter is as follows." Rabbi Moshe felt somewhat better, and he sat up.

"I live in Fostat and the king lives in Cairo, a distance of two *techumei Shabbos*.

"My obligation to the king is very burdensome. Every day, I must see him in the morning. If he is weak, or if one of his children or wives is ill, I spend most of the day in the palace.

"I must also visit the princes every day, and every day one or two ministers are ill.

"If there is nothing unusual, I get back to Fostat in the afternoon. Even before I arrive, I am starving.

"But the corridors are filled with gentiles, important and unimportant people, judges and leaders, a great confusion of people, who are all waiting to see me."

From downstairs, Rabbi Moshe heard someone calling out, "Where is Rabbi Moshe?"

"I don't know, I haven't seen him."

"Go look in the courtyard."

He continued to write. "I dismount from the donkey and wash my hands. Then I ask the patients to please wait until I have eaten a light meal. I only have this one meal, once a day.

"Then I treat the patients and write prescriptions for them. This continues sometimes into the night and some-times—by the faith of the Torah!—until two in the morning.

"I speak to the patients lying on my back from great weariness. When night arrives, I am totally exhausted, too tired even to speak."

Rabbi Moshe sighed.

"I cannot speak with any Jew or spend time with any Jew until *Shabbos*.

"Then all the Jews come to me after the prayers and I guide them regarding what they do during the week. They learn a bit until noon, and then go on their way. Some return and learn again until the evening prayer."

In a letter to a simple man who lived in Fostat and wished to learn Torah from Rabbi Moshe, Rabbi Moshe replied in a letter, "Come to the *beis midrash* on *Shabbos* and you shall perhaps achieve a little of what you want. Perhaps G-d will allow us some time, and we shall learn." (*Igros*)

The room in which Rabbi Moshe sat was bright and colorful—perhaps to make up for the barren monotony of the desert that surrounded Cairo and the sandstone color of the buildings.

Before Rabbi Moshe stood his son, Avraham, scarcely past *bar-mitzvah* age. Rabbi Moshe put down the cameo-cut glass, decorated in red and green, that held a weak wine.

"My son," he said. "My forefathers, to the eighth generation before me, were all rabbis and *dayanim*. G-d willing, after one hundred and twenty years, you shall take my place."

Avraham gazed at his father solemnly.

"You must prepare yourself. You must give yourself over to learning the Torah."

"Yes, Father."

Rabbi Moshe sighed. "Today, the Torah is in exile. Everywhere, it seems, the Torah is being forgotten. In the land of Israel and in Syria—particularly in Aleppo—there are a few sages learning Torah, but not with the total self-sacrifice that is needed.

"In Egypt and in Iraq, there are a few people, here and there—a few grains. Torah has been lost from the children. Most of the great countries are dying, and a few are on the verge of death."

"And Yemen, Father?"

"They have a few men who learn the Talmud—but they do not really understand it. G-d shall give them the reward for learning—but not necessarily for understanding.

"As for North Africa, you know about how the Moslems have destroyed Torah knowledge there."

"Perhaps there are Jews who learn in the far corners of the world," Avraham said.

"Perhaps," said Rabbi Moshe. "But I know that the Jews of India are not familiar with the written Torah. All that they observe is *Shabbos* and *bris milah*. And there are some Moslem lands where the Jews read the Torah according to its simple meaning, without knowing how to interpret it.

"I am weary," Rabbi Moshe admitted. "But I take hope in the thought of the sages of Lunel. They are true Torah scholars. They are men who will carry on the work to the coming generations." (*Igros*)

Rabbi Moshe leaned back. "Now go back to learn, my son." He reached out a feeble hand and gently patted Avraham's hand. Then he drew his hand back and shut his eyes.

In Lunel, Rabbi Yehonasan read the latest letter that Rabbi Moshe had written to him and his colleagues. "You are the only help left, my brothers," wrote Rabbi Moshe. "You are the redeemers. Be strong for the sake of our people. Strive to be warriors, for the matter rests with you.

"Do not rely on me to continue the battle. Today, I can no longer be active, for I am aged—not because I am old, but because my body is so sickly.

"May the Creator help you and make you famous in the land." (*Igros*)

22

Final Years

ON THE SMALL ISLAND OF RODA, THE LONG PILLAR OF THE NILOMETER descended deep into a dark, square well. From the bottom of the well came the rushing noise of the Nile. The stone walls were cool and moist. Descending along the sides of the walls, stone steps without a railing led to the river.

Ibn Assad gazed down into the well, where the flame of an oil lamp descended into the darkness.

The oil lamp swung out to the middle of the well, dimly illuminating the Nilometer. At last, a voice cried up, half-swallowed by the rushing of the water. "Flood level ten cubits!"

Slowly, the oil lamp began to move along the sides of the well, until ibn Assad saw clearly the portly form of Aljarazi carefully ascending the steps, holding on with one hand to the moist wall.

Along the length of the Nilometer, numbers were painted, so that the flood height of the Nile could be exactly determined.

"That's bad," ibn Assad said.

"Too low," Aljarazi agreed, short of breath, as he came to the platform at the top of the well. He blew out the burning wick.

The urchins who worked in the warehouses along the Nile also noticed that the beginning of the summer flood was weak. Alongside the Nile, people had dumped refuse and the carcasses of beasts, and every summer the surging waters of the river washed them away. But this summer, the waters of the Nile barely rose.

The Nile usually swept over the tangled thickets that lay along its borders. But now the meager waters barely lapped at them.

By autumn, the farmers knew that this was going to be a lean year. The water that customarily flooded the fields and poured through the canals was sluggish and shallow.

At the banks, the Nile was green with duckweed and water moss, and became turgid like sludge. A corrupt, impure odor emanated from the Nile, and dead fish floated to the surface.

The people still ate from the old harvest. What could one do? All is in the hands of the All-Merciful.

There was a sharp, whistling sound. At the front of the synagogue, the *shaliach tzibbur* was repeating the *Shemoneh Esrei*. Rabbi Moshe turned to the sound. A Jew in a round, red turban had spit onto the floor of the synagogue, and he was wiping his mouth. He looked at his neighbor, a tall, thick-boned man, who was talking earnestly to him, trying to persuade him of something.

There was another man Rabbi Moshe noticed, a simple

Jew named Yonah. Rabbi Moshe knew that Yonah did not even know how to read the prayers from the *siddur*. He too was talking to a friend.

After the prayers, Rabbi Moshe signalled to Yonah. The man stepped up to the great rabbi.

"Yonah," Rabbi Moshe said, "if you have not yourself recited the silent *Shemoneh Esrei*, you must listen to the *shaliach tzibbur* when he repeats it and recite *Amen* after each blessing."

"Oh?" Yonah hesitated. "I didn't know. I was only doing as everyone else does."

Outside the synagogue, two Moslems passed by, laughing.

"You see that what I said was no exaggeration. That is how the Jews pray: they talk and they spit."

"Praise be the All-Compassionate One Who made us of the true religion."

Their conversation faded into the distance.

Rabbi Moshe turned to his companion, Rabbi Yitzchak. "There must be an end to this talking during the repetition of the *Shemoneh Esrei*!"

Soon, the new decree on prayer by Rabbi Moshe ben Maimon, Chief Rabbi of Egypt, was read aloud in all the synagogues in Fostat and Cairo.

The next morning, the new procedure took effect. In the main synagogue of Fostat, Rabbi Moshe covered his eyes with the rest of the congregation, reciting, *"Shema Yisrael,"* drawing out the *daled* of *Echad* in the ancient pronunciation of a soft "th."

The prayers continued.

"Tzur Yisrael . . . Rock of Israel, rise and help Israel, and redeem, as You have promised, Yehudah and Israel."

The men stood facing the *aron kodesh* and chanted along with the *shaliach tzibbur*. "Redeem us, G-d of Hosts, this is His Name, the Holy One of Israel. (*Yishayahu* 47:4) Blessed are You, O G-d, Who has redeemed Israel."

But now, instead of the silent *Shemoneh Esrei*, the *shaliach* began to recite it aloud: "*Baruch Atah Hashem* . . . Blessed are You, Hashem, our Lord and the Lord of our fathers."

A month later, Rabbi Moshe received a letter from a former student, Rabbi Saadiah ben Rabbi Berachos Hamelamed, who was living in Alexandria. Rabbi Saadiah had heard about this decree and wanted to know more about it.

Rabbi Moshe replied, "When the *shaliach tzibbur* repeats the *Shemoneh Esrei* aloud, all the people who have already prayed and fulfilled their obligation start talking with each other, including conversation about meaningless matters. They turn away from the *aron kodesh* and spit on the ground. It is a disgrace!

"When an unlearned person [who cannot pray on his own behalf] sees this, he will do the same thing. He will leave the synagogue not having fulfilled his prayer obligation.

"That is why I have instituted my decree. There is no more silent prayer. Rather, the *shaliach tzibbur* recites the prayers once, including the *kedushah*. Whoever knows how to pray does so silently along with the *shaliach tzibbur*. And whoever doesn't know the prayer listens attentively to the *shaliach tzibbur*.

"The people bow together with him and face the direction of the *aron kodesh* with the proper intent.

"In this way, everyone fulfills his obligation, and the matter is orderly and correct.

"People do not have to wait patiently through the long repetition of the *Shemoneh Esrei*. And finally, there is no longer desecration of G-d's name that is caused when gentiles see the Jews spitting and talking during the prayers."

The pestilence hit Egypt. The grain sacks in the marketplace sagged emptily, and the miasma from the Nile carried with it decay and ruin.

THE RAMBAM

In the coming summer, the rising waters of the Nile crept up the graduated markings of the Nilometer. The two keepers of the Nilometer looked at each other. "It looks good, Aljarazi!"

By autumn, the clear, heavily flowing water had flooded the fields again. Waterwheels turned, the water glinting in the sunlight, and broad swathes of water coursed through the canals to the rice paddies.

The pestilence was coming to a close.

Going past the tentmakers' bazaar, where textiles in a riot of whirling images were hung out, Rabbi Moshe was taking stock of his life.

What had he accomplished? Had he really changed people? Had he really done what he needed to do in the world? The sky above, stitched with clouds, was the same sky that had hung above the earth when he was born, and it would continue after his death.

How many conflicts had he had? How many times had his reputation, his livlihood or his life been endangered? Why had he been sent down here to earth?

He thought of his son, and he smiled faintly. The boy was growing now. He was a fine, young man. Avraham would take his place one day.

When Rabbi Moshe returned home, Avraham greeted him. Rabbi Moshe's heart was filled with quiet elation. He felt hopeful about the world. Here was a true servant of G-d who could carry the yoke of idealistic, disinterested service. His son would become a true scholar: learned, dispassionate, loving.

In a letter to his former student, Rabbi Yosef ben Rabbi Yehudah, Rabbi Moshe wrote, "When I see the occurrences of the world, I have some consolation in only two things.

"One is when I think about my son, Avraham. The exalted G-d has given him grace and blessing from the blessing of Avraham Avinu.

"Avraham my son is the most modest and humble of people, besides all his other good qualities. He has a good, subtle intelligence and a pleasing nature.

"With G-d's help, he will without a doubt be a great leader among his people.

"I ask G-d to watch him and shower him with compassion." (*Igros* 26)

What was Rabbi Moshe's other consolation?

Perhaps he was glad of how his *Pirush Hamishnayos* had given thousands of people the ability to learn *mishneh* clearly.

Perhaps he thought of his *Mishneh Torah*, a monument of learning and clarity that transformed the Torah literature on *halachah*.

Perhaps he was most concerned with his final work, the *Moreh Nevuchim*, which would be able to occupy the minds and thoughts of thousands of men who might otherwise have considered the Torah not worth their interest.

Or perhaps he thought of his life as a public rabbi, of how he had transformed the Jewish community of Egypt. Here where Jews had been ignorant and overwhelmed by the Karaites, Rabbi Moshe had reduced the Karaites to an inconsequential group. The Rabbinic Jews kept the *mitzvos* with greater enthusiasm and loyalty than they had ever done in living memory.

Perhaps he thought of Yemen, where an entire country of Jews had been so inspired by the words of Rabbi Moshe that, on the brink of mass apostasy and assimilation, they had returned to Torah observance.

Perhaps he thought of Morocco and the letter he had written at the risk of his life that had saved the Jews of that country from despair, conversion to Islam and unnecessary acts of martyrdom.

Perhaps he thought of the scholars of Lunel who had

appreciated his ideas and who could be trusted to continue to spread the influence of Torah learning and observance.

Or perhaps Rabbi Moshe had meant to say that his consolation was his student, Rabbi Yosef, whose *yeshivah* in Baghdad had countered the influence of those who sought to spread poisonous rumors about Rabbi Moshe.

But the words that Rabbi Moshe wrote no longer exist. Only a fragment of his letter survived, in which he expressed the love of his heart for his son, Avraham.

Like Yaakov Avinu, Rabbi Moshe could say of his life, "The years of my life have been few and difficult." (*Bereishis* 47:9) Yet from amidst the adversity and clutter of events that so much interfered with his dedication to the Torah, he created an influence and a Torah literature that has lasted with undiminished immediacy to this day.

The Ramchal writes in *Choker Umekubal* that toward the end of his life, Rabbi Moshe received some Kabbalistic writings. These led him to declare that had he known of this wisdom earlier in his life, he would have spent his time on this and not on philosophy. Other authorities also share this point of view.

There is, however, a piece of evidence that suggests the opposite. In 1201, Rabbi Moshe was asked his opinion of the Kabbalistic sefer, *Shiur Komah*. This work employs strongly anthropological language to speak of G-d's attributes.

In his strong opposition to any description of G-d that might tend to make Him seem physical or divisible into parts, Rabbi Moshe replied, "I have never considered this to be from the Sages. Heaven forbid that it should be from them!

"It is rather nothing else than a work written by a Christian writer.

"In short, it is a great *mitzvah* to destroy this work and wipe out its memory. As the verse says, 'Do not mention the name of other gods.' And to attribute 'height' to G-d is without a doubt under the category of 'other gods.'"

The last years of Rabbi Moshe's life passed. Nothing is known of them. Perhaps now, in his old age, he no longer had to devote his entire time to the medical needs of the vizier and gentile notables.

Perhaps as well, now that he was older, the controversies over his authority were calming down.

On a Sunday night, the twentieth day of *Teves*, 4965 (December 13, 1204), Rabbi Moshe passed away. He was sixty-nine years old.

For three days, the Jews of Fostat mourned.

All the Jews gathered in the synagogue. It was the custom to read from the Torah and the Prophets after the death of an important person.

The Rebuke of Moshe—*Im Bechukosai*—was read. "If you shall walk in My decrees and keep My commandments and do them . . . then I shall give you the rain in its time and the earth shall give its fullness and the tree of the field shall give its fruit." (*Vayikra* 26:3) Rabbi Moshe, who had again presented to the Jews G-d's decrees and commandments, was no more.

The reader now chanted from the beginning of *Yehoshuah*: "Moshe My servant has died. Now arise and pass over this Jordan, you and all this nation, to the land that I give to the children of Israel." (*Yehoshua* 1:2)

For thirty-five years, Rabbi Moshe had lived among the Jews. Now a great gap had been rent in their lives. At the head of the synagogue, amidst the sages, stood Rabbi Moshe's son, Rabbi Avraham, only eighteen years old. Rabbi Avraham would be the next Chief Rabbi and take his father's place at the court of the sultan.

A man had passed from the world who had been more than a giant—for a giant is merely a greater man. Rabbi Moshe had seemed an angel.

Who could have done so much in one lifetime, amidst so

many turbulent moments and so many burdens of time? Rabbi Moshe had contained within himself worlds of Torah, faith, science and knowledge.

For seven days, Rabbi Moshe's body lay in a sunken room in his apartment. The house where Rabbi Moshe lived was later turned into a synagogue, and the place where his holy body lay is still considered holy. An eternal lamp burns there. Whoever is troubled or ill prays there that he be treated mercifully in the merit of the *tzaddik*.

The Moslems too mourned, for they had esteemed Rabbi Moshe as one of the greatest sages of the time.

The Jews, who were stunned by the great loss, eventually called this year *"Nehi Nihyah"*—"Groans of mourning". (*Michah* 2:4) The numerical value of *nehi* is sixty-five, the date of Rabbi Moshe's death, and the numerical value of *nihyah* is seventy, his age (approximately).

Eight days after Rabbi Moshe's passing, the news arrived in Jerusalem. Here too the Jews mourned deeply. It was partially due to Rabbi Moshe's efforts that Saladin had let them return to Jerusalem and live there peacefully.

They fasted and eulogized the great rabbi of the age. All the *sifrei Torah* were taken out. After the reading of *Im Bechukosai*, the passage from *Shmuel I* was read, about the loss of the holy ark: "The wife of Pinchas said, 'The glory of Israel has gone into exile . . .The glory has left Israel, for the ark of G-d has been taken.'" (*Shmuel I* 4:21-22)

Rabbi Moshe's body was carried up through the Sinai and the Negev, and buried in Tiverias.

According to legend, Bedouins attacked the funeral procession in the desert, believing Rabbi Moshe's casket to contain a treasure. When they could not move the casket, they realized that this is the body of a holy man, and they themselves joined the procession, protecting the Jews from harm.

The camel that carried Rabbi Moshe's casket continued the rest of the journey unguided, until he reached Tiverias and knelt. Then the Jews knew that Rabbi Moshe should be buried there.

Rabbi Maimon is said to be buried in Tiverias. (Rabbi Chaim Vital, as quoted in *Harambam*, by N. T. Sifrai, p. 266) It is reasonable to assume that Rabbi Moshe's body was carried this great distance so he could lay next to his father.

For many years, the area surrounding the graves of Rabbi Moshe and Rabbi Maimon (where Rabbi Yochanan ben Zakai is also buried) was neglected.

The land was bought from Arab owners and a new tombstone put in place in 1927.

During the excavation, the tombstone of Rabbi Moshe's grandson, Rabbi David, was discovered as well.

Rabbi Moshe's original tombstone is inscribed with the legend, "Here is buried our rabbi, Moshe ben Maimon, the choicest of mankind."

A second tombstone says, "The Rambam, born 14 *Nissan*, 4895, passed away 20 *Teves* 4965, the Strong Hand, the Teacher of the Perplexed."

A third tombstone bears the famous slogan, "From Moshe to Moshe, none arose like Moshe."

There are some men who are so great that they transcend the idea of personality. Their character is so noble, their ability so vast and so realized that they acquire the nature of an elemental force.

Rabbi Moshe was such a man. He was nobility; he was selfless love for others; he was the knowledge of Torah.

The facets of Rabbi Moshe's accomplishments form a mosaic, like the brilliant mosaics in Rabbi Moshe's Cordoba, Fez and Fostat.

But even when the mosaic is pieced together, one sees that its surface is curiously illusory. Behind the descriptions, one senses, are ever greater depths, doubled and quintupled images of increasing profundity, fading into an indeterminate distance.

The more one knows of Rabbi Moshe, the more does one love what he embodied: wisdom, mature knowledge, and the spirit of the Torah in its deepest, most compassionate and most monumental aspects.

Glossary

Aggadah: homiletics
apikores: apostate
aron kodesh: holy ark containing Torah scrolls
bar-mitzvah: *halachic* adulthood
beis din: rabbinical court
beis midrash: study hall
bimah: pulpit
bris milah: covenant of cicumcision
Chanukah: Festival of Lights
cholent: special *Shabbos* stew
dayan: rabbinical judge

gadol hador: greatest of the generation
Gemara: part of the Talmud
geonim: Talmudic geniuses
halachah: Jewish law
Havdalah: concluding ritual of *Shabbos*
Kaddish: mourner's prayer
kashrus: state of being kosher
kedushah: holiness
melavah malkah: post-*Shabbos* meal
mesorah: tradition

mezuzah: scroll affixed to doorpost

mikveh: ritual bath

Minchah: afternoon service

minyan: quorom of ten

Mishlei: Book of Proverbs

Mishneh (Mishnayos): part(s) of the Talmud

mitzvah: Torah commandment

motzei Shabbos: night after the *Shabbos*

Pesach: Passover, early spring festival

Pirkei Avos: Chapters of the Father, Talmudic ethical tractate

Purim: Festival of Lots

rosh yeshivah: dean

Seder: Passover feast

sefer: book

selichos: penitential prayers

shaliach tzibbur: cantor

Shalom aleichem: peace unto you; greeting

Shavuos: Pentecost, late spring festival

Shemoneh Esrei: the Eighteen Benedictions, fundamental part of daily prayers

shiur: lecture

shochet: ritual slaughterer

Shulchan Aruch: Code of Jewish Law

siddur: prayer book

sugya: Talmudic topic

sukkah: *Sukkos* booth

Sukkos: Festival of Tabernacles, autumn festival

tallis: prayer shawl

talmid chacham: Torah scholar

Talmud: the Oral law

Tanach: the Scriptures

techias hameisim: resurrection of the dead

tefillin: phylacteries

Tehillim: Book of Psalms

tzaddik: righteous person

yeshivah: Torah school

Yom Kippur: Day of Atonement

zemer: song